PUBLISHER 2003

BRIAN AUSTIN

In easy steps is an imprint of Computer Step
Southfield Road . Southam
Warwickshire CV47 0FB . United Kingdom
www.ineasysteps.com

Notice of Liability
Every effort has been made to ensure that this book contains
accurate and current information. However, Computer Step and the
author shall not be liable for any loss or damage suffered by readers
as a result of any information contained herein.

Trademarks
Microsoft® and Windows® are registered trademarks of Microsoft
Corporation. All other trademarks are acknowledged as belonging to
their respective companies.

Printed and bound in the United Kingdom

ISBN-13 978-1-84078-277-6
ISBN-10 1-84078-277-3

Table of Contents

Creating web page forms 163

Previewing and publishing your website 171

Research and translation services 181

Index 187

Publisher basics

Thank you for using this book and welcome to Publisher 2003 in easy steps. Chapter One provides a brief introduction to this exciting and amazingly powerful print and web design program. Enjoy!

Covers

Chapter One

Activating and starting Publisher

At any time while using Publisher, you can easily access a range of different Help options and information. To get started, choose Microsoft Office Publisher Help from the Help menu, and press the F1 function key.

Activating your copy of Publisher

Like all Microsoft Office applications, you'll need to activate your Publisher installation. You can use the step-by-step wizard to help you activate your copy quickly, via the Internet or over the telephone. Plus, the Activate Product command is always available on the Help menu. To activate Publisher, you'll need the program's product key that comes with your copy.

To start Publisher

On the Windows Task bar, click the Start button, then on the menu options, click on All Programs, followed by Microsoft Office, and Microsoft Office Publisher 2003. Publisher then shows the Start-up window containing the task pane – a special window to provide quick access to the most popular commands (see facing page). In the task pane, you can choose one of several options to start a new publication or open an existing document.

Although you can use Publisher for a limited period without activating your copy, if you wait too long, your copy will go into Reduced Functionality Mode, until you choose to do so. Therefore, aim to activate your copy as soon as possible after installation.

You can also choose to register your copy with Microsoft, to stay informed about updates, special offers, etc. While registration is optional, product activation is essential.

About web mode and print mode

Publisher can help you create professionally designed publications for both print and the web. Depending upon which type of publication you're working on, Publisher chooses either web mode or print mode. The commands Publisher makes available depend on which mode you're in. For example, commands to create web page navigation bars are not available in print mode.

In Publisher, after you create a publication in print mode, you can usually convert that document to web mode. Likewise, you can easily convert a web page publication into a print publication.

To convert a print publication to a web publication, open the File menu, click Convert to Web Publication and follow the instructions given in the wizard.

When you convert one type of publication into another, Publisher copies all the text and graphics over to the new publication. Sometimes however, depending on the document content, you may still need to perform some final formatting changes once the conversion has taken place, in order to create a polished publication.

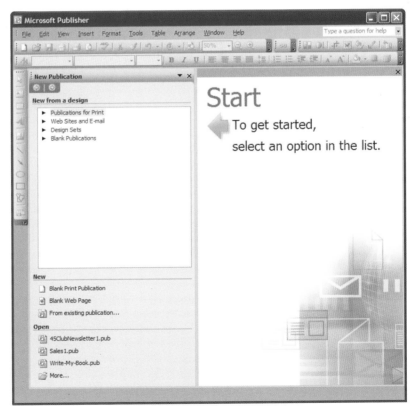

Publisher now provides lots of options for users with disabilities: type "accessibility" in the online Help system to find out more.

Introducing Publisher wizards

We'll look at opening existing publications and creating your own publications from the beginning later in this book. For now, let's take a brief look at wizards.

A Publisher wizard does most of the hard work of designing the layout of your publication for you, while still giving you a lot of control over how your publication will eventually look. You simply make your choices at each stage, and you can even go back to previous stages to try out other designs. Even if you've already chosen a wizard-based design, you can still edit it to suit your needs whenever you wish.

You can display or hide the task pane at any time. Here's how: simply open the View menu and choose task pane.

To start a wizard, click Open on the File menu and click the New command. By default, Publisher displays the New Publication task pane on the left side of the screen. Under New from a design, Publisher provides lots wizards to help you create a publication quickly.

To quickly choose and start a wizard design or style, simply double-click the wizard icon you want in the right-side pane, and follow the instructions Publisher provides.

If more designs are available than Publisher can currently display, you can use the scroll bar and buttons on the right, to bring the remaining options into view.

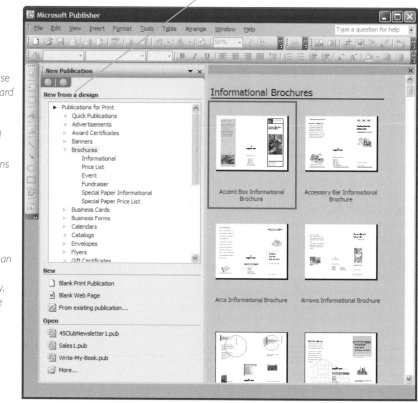

Getting to know the Publisher screen

When you start Publisher, by default, the New Publication task pane displays on the left side of the main Publisher window.

From the New Publication task pane, you can access commands and options to start, open, view, edit and save your publication. Or, you can use the equivalent commands on the menus. We'll explore these main commands throughout this book.

When you're starting with Publisher from scratch, here's a quick way to identify each toolbar. Simply place your mouse pointer anywhere on a toolbar and right-click. On the floating menu that appears, a displayed toolbar is shown with a tick mark next to its name. Click any name to place or remove its tick mark and correspondingly, display or hide its toolbar.

To quickly learn more about a tool on a toolbar, position the mouse pointer directly on top of the desired tool. Publisher then names the tool in the form of a ToolTip – a label that briefly describes the purpose of the tool.

The screenshots in this guide are taken using Windows XP. If you're using an older version of Windows, the screens on your version may differ.

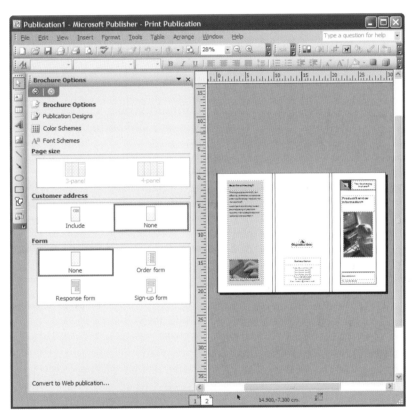

Introducing Publisher's powerful toolbars

Like any other Microsoft Office application, Publisher provides a variety of toolbars, that contain one-click buttons for quick access to the most popular commands. By default, the horizontal Standard toolbar and Formatting toolbar are usually placed just under the menu names, and the vertical Objects toolbar on the upper left side of the screen. When you click some buttons, Publisher may display other tools or toolbars to give more choices.

Selecting, copying, moving and pasting

In Publisher, you select something if you want to affect or work on the selected item in a particular way. For example, to change the size and proportions of a drawn rectangle, you must select the rectangle first. Only then can you change the height, width, or both, or modify the rectangle. When you click an object, usually, you'll use the Select Objects tool on the Objects toolbar, to select the object. Publisher then places selection handles around the selected object as shown on the selected box here.

With the Select Objects tool active on the Objects toolbar, to select several objects at the same time, drag a rectangular selection box around the objects you want to select.

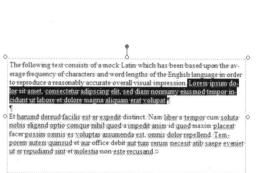

Selecting text

You can also select text by dragging across the text you want with the left mouse button. Publisher also refers to this action as highlighting the text you want to work on.

To select all objects in the Publisher window in a single action, open the Edit menu and click Select All. To clear the selection, click anywhere outside of a selected object.

Introducing master pages

If the object you want to select does not appear to be selectable, the object may have been placed on a master page. A master page is where we put items that we want to repeat – like headers, footers and perhaps a logo. To quickly move to a master page, press the Ctrl+M keys. This is a shortcut way of opening the View menu and clicking the Master Page command. Press Ctrl+M again to return to your normal Publisher page. See Chapter 8 for more details about master pages.

The following text consists of a mock Latin which has been based upon the average frequency of characters and word lengths of the English language in order to reproduce a reasonably accurate overall visual impression. Lorem ipsum dolor sit amet, consectetur adipscing elit, sed diam nonnumy eiusmod tempor incidunt ut labore et dolore magna aliquam erat volupat.

Et harumd dereud facilis est er expedit distinct. Nam liber a tempor cum soluta nobis eligend optio comque nihil quod a impedit anim id quod maxim placeat facer possim omnis es voluptas assumenda est, omnis dolor repellend. Temporem autem quinsud et aur office debit aut tum rerum necesit atib saepe eveniet ut er repudiand sint et molestia non este recusand.

If the object you want to select is behind or underneath another larger object, first, select the largest object (the one nearest to you), then choose the Send Backward or the Send to Back commands on the Arrange > Order menu. Repeat, until the object you want is in front.

Moving, copying, cutting and pasting objects

To move an object, first select the object you want to move as described above, then drag it to the required position. To copy, cut and paste text and graphic objects select the text or object you want, then open the Edit menu and choose the Cut, Copy and Paste commands, as is standard within Windows.

Moving around a publication

Publisher provides a variety of simple, but powerful tools to enable you to move in and around your publication.

If your publication is made up of more than a single page, and you're seeing your pages in Single page view, you can choose to view adjacent pages side-by-side, by opening the View menu and choosing the Two-Page Spread command.

The scroll bars

Click the horizontal or vertical scroll buttons on the horizontal and vertical scroll bars to scroll the publication page up or down, and left or right.

The page control buttons

To move to a desired page, click the page button you want on the lowermost left-hand corner of the Publisher window. See the illustration below:

To quickly move to a specific page in your publication, press the F5 key, then enter the page number you want in the Go to page box and press ENTER to finish.

Zooming in or out

To move a selected object closer or further away, use the Zoom In and Zoom Out buttons next to the Zoom box, situated on the Standard toolbar (see below). Or, you can enter a percentage in the Zoom box. Or click the down-arrow button next to the Zoom box, and click the value you want. To quickly change between the current zoom setting and the actual size of the object, press the F9 key.

If you select an object before you zoom in or out, any following zoom action is centered on the selected object, rather than the entire page.

Undo and Redo

In the Edit menu and in button form on the Standard toolbar, Publisher provides two commands that allow you to undo or redo most last actions – useful if you make a mistake. Click Undo to reverse the most recent editing action or command you chose. Redo simply reverses your most recent Undo. The Edit menu commands are sometimes better in that they can provide more precise information about the type of object, you want the Undo/Redo action to change.

Most actions can be undone in Publisher. If Undo is available, choose Undo as soon as you're aware of your mistake, ideally, before pressing any key or clicking a mouse button elsewhere.

Starting a publication

From the task pane, Publisher provides five main ways in which you can start a publication. You can opt to:

- start a publication for print using a wizard

- create a website or e-mail publication using a wizard

- build a document using a series of specific design set styles

- choose a blank document and select from a series of page sizes and types – and perform the entire page design yourself

- open an existing Publisher document

A wizard approach – as shown in the illustration below – can help you create a new web or print publication based on a predesigned interactive template. The wizard asks some simple questions, then creates the basic layout for you based on your answers.

If you create and save a publication as a template, you can easily create a new publication based on the template you saved. Here's how: simply open the File menu and click New, then in the task pane, choose the template you want from the list of templates shown under the Templates list.

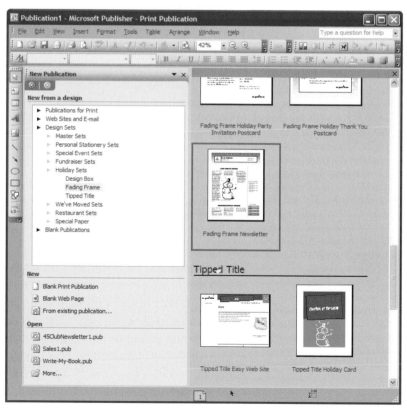

Choosing where to print

You can create a variety of different publications in Publisher, including commercial grade print publications and websites. For print publications however, you may have several choices as to how to create the final product. Consider the guidelines below.

Printing to a desktop printer

Desktop printing is usually inexpensive compared to the options below, providing only a few copies are needed. Also, you maintain full control, the entire process can be fun and you can learn much.

However, if you want high quality output, desktop printing may not may not be your best choice. If your publication requires a top quality finish, any special treatment, such as metallic inks, glossy finish, etc., then you local copy shop or commercial printing provider may be your best or only option. As a minimum, you need a desktop printer that is capable of printing at the resolution and quality you want. Finally, you'll have to consider running costs, paper, ink or toner, and optionally binding requirements.

Copy shop

You local copy shop may be ideal for printing a publication that requires many copies at average-to-good print quality. They can also be amazingly quick. Providing you order sufficient copies, prices too can be one of the most attractive points. Many copy shops also provide folding, trimming, binding and stapling services.

However, copy shop printing can be a more expensive option for lower quantities. As the publication goes out of your hands, you also loose some control, quality may not be as good as you want in some instances, and you'll need to consider how to deliver your Publisher file to your chosen copy shop.

Commercial

With commercial printing, the highest quality output can be achieved. Many commercial printers may also include a wide range of speciality options like embossing, metallic inks, Print On Demand (POD), etc. Commercial printing can be ideal providing large quantities of a publication are required. Folding, trimming, binding and stapling services should also be on offer. You'll also need to consider how to deliver your Publisher file to your chosen printing service provider.

Establish where you're going to print your publication, before you start. Different models of desktop printer provide different options. If you lay out a publication for one printer, then change the target printer later, you may have a considerable amount of re-work to do.

Opening a publication

Publisher provides several ways to open a publication. You can click the File menu, and then click the Open command. In the Open Publication dialog box, under the Look in list, choose the drive, folder or Internet address where the file you want is located. You can navigate to the file you want, click the Publication document, then click the Open button.

To view file properties on a currently opened file, open the File menu and click Properties.

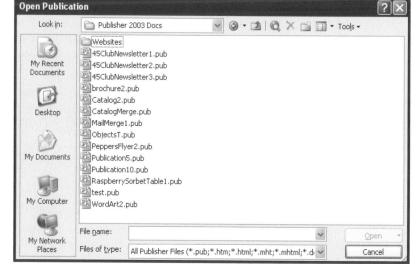

If you want to open a copy or a read-only version of a publication rather than the publication file itself, instead of clicking the Open button, click the down-arrow button next to it and click Open as Copy if available, or Open Read-Only. Remember, a read-only version can only be viewed, not changed. You can also open a publisher file by clicking the Open button on the Standard toolbar.

Or, if the publication you want has been opened recently, in the File menu, Publisher stores a list of shortcuts to recently opened files, which you can click to open the file. Furthermore, with the New Publication or Getting started task pane displayed, Publisher lists several of the most recently opened files, which you can click to quickly open the file you want.

Using publication design sets

A design set is a collection of components with a consistent look and feel, which you can use to create a common identity across a range of publication types.

To create a publication from a design set, open the File menu and click New. In the New Publication task pane, under the section New from a design, click Design Sets. Click the design you want in the task pane. On the right side, click the publication type you want. Publisher creates your publication. You can apply further choices – see margin tips for additional options at this stage.

An example design set could include templates to create a business card, brochure, letterhead, newsletter and website, that all have the same look and feel.

By choosing and applying a Publisher design set to your business, you can help create your own brand. Publisher provides 45 superb professionally designed master design sets, plus a range of other standard design sets.

In the task pane, once you've chosen your publication type, and if it is a web page, newsletter or catalog, Publisher provides a Page Content link, from where you can change or choose additional options.

For all publication types: to change the basic design, click Publication Designs; to change the color scheme, click Color Schemes; to change the fonts used, click Font Schemes. Each option chosen leads to more choices.

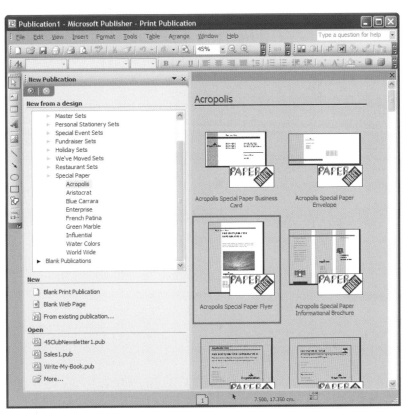

In your publication, click each text and graphic placeholder and replace with your own content. When ready, open the File menu and click Save As. In the Save As dialog box, click or move to the folder where you want to save your publication. In the File name box, type a name for your new publication, and click Save.

Working with Publisher frames

After you've drawn a text frame, you can start entering text immediately – just start typing. If you want to zoom in to the frame, click inside the frame with the right mouse button, then from the floating menu, click Zoom, followed by the Selected Objects command.

Introducing objects

Until now, we've referred to objects in the general sense. However, in Publisher, the term object has a more precise meaning. An object is simply any independently movable item which you can place and move about on the workspace – for example, a text box, table, or a picture (see Chapter 2 for more information). Most objects in Publisher are placed onto the page using the tools on the Objects toolbar.

Introducing frames

Publisher uses frames to hold objects making moving objects around easier. Publisher uses different types of frame to hold different page design elements such as text, pictures, tables, WordArt (see margin) and Publisher's own store of pictures, sounds and other objects in the Design Gallery.

A frame is an object and as such, can be manipulated in various ways.
Objects are examined in more detail in Chapter 2.

When you want to place something on the page, sometimes, Publisher automatically creates the frame for you, depending on which command you choose. In other instances, before you can place the design element you want on a page, you'll need to create a frame to hold the object – an easy task. All frames can be resized, moved and aligned precisely using guide lines and ruler marks, and even aligned to other objects on the page.

The frame tools

To create frames in Publisher, you use the tools situated on the Objects toolbar, as shown below:

WordArt is a program which is available in Publisher if you want to apply some fancy effects to text using different font styles and so on, like this:

Text Box tool
Insert Table tool
Insert WordArt tool
Picture Frame tool

Clip Art
Picture from File
Empty Picture Frame
From Scanner or Camera...

Additional picture commands available when you click the Picture Frame tool

To create a frame

To draw the size and position of your frame accurately, watch the mouse pointer Object Position and Object Size indicators on the lower right of the main Publisher window, as you draw your frame.

1 On the Objects toolbar, click the tool you want: the mouse pointer symbol changes to a crosshair shape.

2 Place the mouse pointer where you want the left-hand corner of your frame to be situated.

3 Press and hold down the left mouse button while you drag the mouse diagonally down the page to form the bottom right-hand corner of your frame.

A selected frame has several small black boxes positioned around its perimeter – these are the selection handles, which you can use to change the size, shape and position of the object.

4 When the frame size and shape are correct, release the mouse button: Publisher identifies your frame with a non-printing light outline as shown in the illustrations below.

To drag a ruler onto the page, simply place the mouse pointer on to a ruler, then press and hold down the Shift key. The mouse pointer changes to a double-arrow symbol. Then, drag the desired ruler onto the page. When finished, simply repeat to drag the ruler back to its origin.

To move or delete a frame

Hold down the mouse button anywhere on a frame perimeter but not on a selection handle. When the mouse pointer changes to crossed arrows, drag the frame to where you want. To delete a frame, click anywhere inside the frame and press the Delete key.

To resize a frame

You can resize a selected frame by changing its width, height, or both width and height at the same time, by dragging a selection handle. To keep the original frame proportions, press and hold down the Shift key while you resize a frame using a corner selection handle. Or, if you want to keep the center of the frame in the original position, use the Ctrl key instead.

Flowing text into text boxes

Once text has been flowed into multiple text boxes, you can track the flow sequence from one text box to the next, by clicking the Go To Next Text Box and Go To Previous Text Box buttons, on the right-hand side of the Connect Text Boxes toolbar, as shown on this page.

Where you have multiple connected text boxes, if you want to disconnect a text box from the others, first click in any connected text box (other than the last one in the sequence), then choose the Break Forward Link button on the Connect Text Boxes toolbar, as shown below.

If after inserting "Continue on Page XX" labels you change your mind, you can remove these labels simply by clearing the desired check boxes in the Format Text Box dialog box and then clicking OK.

Let's assume you've drawn a text box. You can then start typing text directly into the text box. When there is more text in a text box than can be viewed, the Text Overflow symbol ([A ···]) appears. To flow the remaining text, first draw another text box where you want, either on the same page or another page.

Then, click in the first text box from which you want to flow the hidden text. Next, click the Create Text Box Link button on the Connect Text Boxes toolbar. Finally, move to where you new text box is, and place your mouse pointer inside the new text box you just created – the mouse pointer changes to a pouring pitcher symbol, like this: ✋. Click in the text box to flow the excess text.

Publisher now does three key actions: (1) pours the remaining text into the second text box, (2) places a Go To Next Text Box button at the bottom of the first text box, and (3) places a Go To Previous Text Box button at the top of this second text box (shown opposite). The Go To … buttons are only visible in the text box containing the text cursor.

Including "Continued on page ..." notices

To help your readers follow the text flow, you can insert "Continued on page XX" and "Continued from page XX" labels. Here's how. Right-click on a linked text box, then from the floating menu, click Format Text Box.

In the Format Text Box dialog box, click the Text Box tab. Under Text autofitting, click one or both Include "Continued on page ..." and Include "Continued from page ..." check boxes, and click OK. Repeat the above for each connected text box in the sequence.

The following text consists of a mock Latin which has been based upon the average frequency of characters and word lengths of the English language in order to reproduce a reasonably accurate overall visual impression. Lorem ipsum dolor sit amet, consectetur adipscing elit, sed diam nonnumy eiusmod tempor incidunt ut labore et dolore magna aliquam erat volupat.

Et harumd dereud facilis est er expedit distinct. Nam liber a tempor cum soluta nobis eli-

gend optio comque nihil quod a impedit anim id quod maxim placeat facer possim omnis es voluptas assumenda est, omnis dolor repellend. Temporem autem quinsud et aur office debit aut tum rerum necesit atib saepe

Saving and closing Publisher

The Save button on the Standard toolbar looks like this:

To set Publisher to save your publication automatically while you work, first, open the Tools menu, click Options, and then click Save. Click to select the Save AutoRecover info every check box. Then in the minutes box, choose how often you want Publisher to save.

Once you've named and saved a publication, to quickly save it without using the menus or toolbar, simply press Ctrl+S, instead if you wish.

When you save a publication as a template, the Templates list in the task pane won't be shown until you have saved at least one publication as a template, and then closed and restarted Publisher.

To save a publication

You can either click the Save button on the Standard toolbar, or open the File menu and click Save. If you're saving a publication for the first time, Publisher will prompt you to name your file in the Save As dialog box. In the File name box, type a name for your publication, choose where you want to store it, then click the Save button.

After you've saved your publication once, the next time you save, Publisher already knows the filename and so will not display the Save As dialog box again – unless you choose to save your publication to another name, by clicking the Save As command in the File menu.

Closing Publisher and exiting Publisher

To close the current Publisher document, open the File menu and click Close. If the document has not been saved, Publisher prompts you to save, as outlined above.

To exit Publisher, open the File menu and click Exit. If you have an open publication when you choose the Exit command, Publisher closes the document before exiting the program.

To exit Publisher quickly, press Alt+F4. However, if the document has not been saved, Publisher prompts you to save it before exiting.

Some Publisher extras

To change the default folder for storing Publisher publications

While working with Windows programs and surfing the web, you may need to perform a lot of up/down scrolling and dragging. To ease strain on your hands, consider using a mouse that has a center wheel that can be used to scroll much more easily.

Publisher normally saves to the My Documents folder. However, you can set the default folder to somewhere else. Open the Tools menu and click Options, followed by the General tab. Under File locations, click to highlight the entry for Publications, then click Modify. In the Modify Location dialog box, you can select another folder, or create a new folder where you want. Click OK twice.

Using Microsoft Office Document Scanning and Imaging

Microsoft Office Document is made up of two parts: Microsoft Office Document Scanning and Microsoft Office Document Imaging. Microsoft Office Document Scanning is used in connection with a compatible scanner, if you have one installed. Microsoft Office Document Imaging helps you manage and work with scanned documents easily. You can use both components to scan, read, manage and manipulate a range of scanned documents and to perform Optical Character Recognition (OCR).

If you click the right mouse button while the mouse pointer is placed over several selected objects, the command you choose applies to all the selected objects. For example, using this method, you can delete multiple objects quickly.

To start either program, click the following sequence: Start > All Programs > Microsoft Office > Microsoft Office Tools > then choose either Microsoft Office Document Scanning or Microsoft Office Document Imaging.

Working with handwriting recognition

You would use handwriting recognition in any Microsoft Office program in which you wanted to enter text by hand instead of typing. You can use a graphics tablet to write, a pen tablet, your mouse, or another compatible option. Microsoft Office converts your handwritten material to typed characters and inserts them into a standard text box.

Handwriting recognition is a feature of specific versions of Microsoft Office (Simplified Chinese, Traditional Chinese, English, Japanese, and Korean). For more information, see your Microsoft Office manual.

To install handwriting recognition into Windows, open the Control Panel and click Add or Remove Programs. In the Currently installed programs list, click Microsoft Office 2003, followed by Change. Click Add or Remove Features, then click Next. In the Custom Setup screen, click to select Choose advanced customization of applications. Click Next. In the Office Shared Features, click expand. Near Handwriting, click the down-arrow button, then Run from My Computer. Finally, click Update.

Introducing objects

In Chapter 2, we explore one of the most important terms in Publisher: objects. You can discover how to move and manipulate objects and how to draw and work with simple shapes in Publisher.

Covers

Chapter Two

Using Format Painter

You can copy a selected object using the Copy and Paste commands in the Edit menu, or from the pop-up menu when you click the right mouse button on a selected object.

However, sometimes you may only want to copy the formatting of an object, not the object itself. Publisher provides a quick and easy way to do exactly that. Here's how. Select the object whose formatting you want to copy, then carry out the steps below:

1   On the Standard toolbar, click the Format Painter button.

2   As you move the mouse pointer back onto the page, the mouse pointer changes to a paintbrush symbol.

You can also use *Format Painter to copy text formatting from one text object to another. First, click in the text frame whose formatting you want to copy. Then perform the steps described on this page.*

3   Now perform either Step 4 or Step 5.

4   To copy the formatting of the selected object to another single object, with the loaded paintbrush mouse pointer, simply click the desired target object.

Rectangle

5   (Optional) If you want to copy the formatting to several objects, click-and-drag a selection box around the objects to which you want to copy formatting. When you release the mouse pointer, Publisher copies the formatting to the objects you specified.

Resizing objects

You can easily change the size of any single object or group of objects at any time. When you resize a group of objects, Publisher can temporarily configure the group as a single object.

To resize an object, first click the object you want. Publisher then places selection handles around the selected object. Next, place your mouse pointer over a selection handle and perform Step 1 or Step 2 or Step 3 below, before completing Step 4:

To resize using the object center as the reference point, hold down Ctrl while you drag a corner selection handle. Then release the mouse button before you release the Ctrl key.

1 To change the height, drag the middle-top or middle-bottom selection handle.

2 To change the width, use the middle-left or middle-right selection handle.

To constrain the resizing action both proportionally and centrally, hold down both Shift and Ctrl keys as you resize, but release the mouse button before you release Shift and Ctrl.

3 To change both height and width at the same time, use a corner selection handle.

4 When the mouse pointer symbol changes to a Resizer symbol, drag to resize the object to the desired size.

When you've selected items to move or resize by dragging, remember, you can also click the right mouse button over the selection to display commands for manipulating objects.

To resize a text frame or custom shape keeping to the original proportions, hold down the Shift key as you resize, but release the mouse button before you release Shift. To resize a picture in the same way, simply perform the action in Step 3 above.

Resizing a group of objects

To resize several objects at the same time, hold down Shift while you click each object you want to resize. Next, click the Group Objects button at the lower right corner of the selection. Then, perform Steps 2 or 3 above and resize as required. Click the Group Objects button again to ungroup the objects. You can discover more about grouping and ungrouping objects on page 29.

Rotating objects

To quickly rotate an object accurately to any angle from 0 to 360 degrees, perform the steps below:

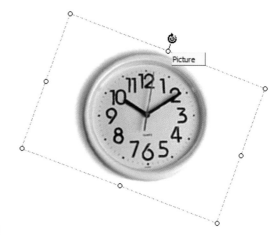

1 Click the object you want to rotate.

2 Position the mouse pointer on a selection handle. When the mouse pointer symbol changes to the Rotate symbol drag the mouse in the direction you want to rotate.

If you change your mind after rotating, click Undo in the Edit menu.

To rotate a group of objects at the same time
First, make sure all the objects you want to rotate are selected. You can use the multiple object selecting method using the Shift key, as described on the previous page.

To rotate an object by 90 degrees
Simply open the Arrange menu, click Rotate or Flip, then choose the option you want.

To unrotate a rotated object
If you want to reverse a rotated object, after selecting the object, open the Arrange menu and choose Rotate or Flip, followed by Custom Rotate. Then click the No Rotation button, followed by the Close button.

When you position the mouse pointer on a selection handle to rotate an object, if the Rotate symbol does not appear, make sure that you held down Alt before placing the mouse pointer on the handle.

To flip an object
Flipping an object in a horizontal direction, is like creating a mirror image. Flipping vertically, turns an object upside down.

To flip the object you want, open the Arrange menu and click Rotate or Flip. Then choose either Flip Horizontal or Flip Vertical.

Centering and aligning objects

Publisher provides several options to make the job of aligning objects on the page easy. To quickly align objects in relation to each other, or the margin guides, first hold down Shift while you select all the objects you want to align. Next, open the Arrange menu, click Align or Distribute. Then, click the alignment option you want in the alignment submenu.

To draw an object from its center outwards, press and hold down the Ctrl key before you choose the desired drawing tool. Next, draw your shape and then release the mouse button before releasing the Ctrl key.

You can also move a selected object in small steps by using the Nudge command in the Arrange menu (or press Alt and click the Up Arrow, Down Arrow, Left Arrow or Right Arrow keys).

Here's how to change the nudge objects distance. Open the Tools menu, click Options, then the Edit tab. Select the check box: Arrow keys nudge object by, then enter the distance you want in the edit box. Click OK.

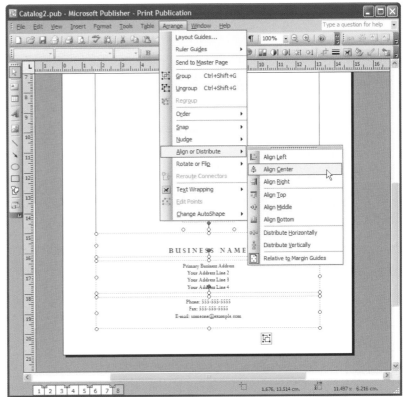

Aligning in relation to margin guides

Perform the steps listed above to select the objects you want, and display the Align or Distribute command – except this time, click the Relative to Margin Guides command first. Then, choose the Align ... option you want in the same submenu. For example, to align all selected objects vertically in the center of the page, you would now choose Align Center. The icons next to each command provide a snapshot of what each command does.

Moving objects around

Moving one or more objects in Publisher is simple. You may want to move objects around the current page, from the page to the scratch-pad gray workspace, or from page to page. To move an object, perform the following steps:

During Step 1, if you can't select the object by clicking it, the object may be hidden behind another (transparent) object. Here's what to do. Click any object, then press Tab or Shift+Tab in sequence, until the object you want is selected.

1 Click the object you want to move. Publisher then places selection handles around the selected object.

2 Place the mouse pointer over the selected object or on the object's perimeter (but not on a selection handle).

You cannot move highlighted text using this technique, as highlighted text is not an object. However, you can use the standard Windows Cut and Paste commands instead.

3 When the mouse pointer changes to the Mover symbol, drag the object to where you want.

4 Release the left mouse button.

Moving several objects at a time

One way to move several objects together is to hold down Shift as you click each object you want to move, and move the mouse pointer over the selection until the Mover symbol appears, then drag to the new location as described above. To constrain the movement to the horizontal or vertical directions only, continue holding down Shift until the objects are in the new position and you have released the mouse button.

The empty workspace region or scratch-pad gray area outside of the paper in the Publisher window, is an ideal place to temporarily store or move an object. The scratch-pad area occupies the same space and location, for every page in your publication.

A note about placing inline objects

You can place an object within a line of text, in a space that is normally occupied by text. Then, Publisher refers to it as an inline object. See Publisher Help for details: enter "inline object".

Grouping and ungrouping objects

Sometimes, you may want to work with several objects at the same time, without disturbing the position or spacing of the individual objects in relation to each other.

 Another way to select multiple objects you want to group is to press and hold down the Shift key while you click on each object individually.

Publisher provides a smart way in which these objects can be treated as a one item while you move, resize or rotate the group in a single action. Publisher refers to this procedure as grouping. You can group or ungroup objects at any time.

To group and ungroup several objects, perform the following steps:

1 Hold down the left mouse button and drag a selection box around the objects you want to group.

 To identify at a glance if an object is grouped, look at the selection handles. Grouped objects have one set of selection handles around the group.

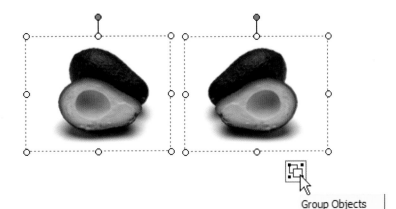

Group Objects

 To select a single object within a group, with which to perform some formatting task to the selected object, hold down Shift while you click the object you want.

2 Click the Group Objects button.

3 To ungroup the selection, click the group to select it, then click the Group Objects button again.

4 Click anywhere outside of the selection to clear the boundary box.

Layering objects

To create the illusion of depth, you can place several overlapping objects on a page. The last object placed appears to be closest to us, while the first object placed seems furthest away, and so on.

Publisher refers to this condition as layering, and to a group of layered objects, collectively, as the stack. Referring to the two example photo objects below, the larger photo of the peppers is considered to be situated at the back or bottom of the stack.

To change the order of layered objects, follow the steps below:

You can also change the layering of more than one object at a time, by first selecting all the objects you want to change. To do this, hold down the Shift key while you click each object you want.

| Click the object you want to change.

To ensure text or pictures appear behind all objects on every page in your publication, place the objects you want on a master page (see page 106).

2 Open the Arrange menu, click the Order command, followed by one of the following commands from the submenu that displays. Depending on what you want to do, click Bring to Front, or Bring Forward, or Send Backward, or Send to Back.

To overlay text onto another object, drag out a text box, type and format your text, then place it in front of the object. Arrange the order of layering. To see an object through a text box, select the text box and click Ctrl+T.

Applying and changing borders

Borders, although simple, can be ideal to help make a picture stand out, or help focus the eye towards an object, or text content. You can easily add, modify or delete a border around a text or graphic object. Furthermore, with rectangular borders, you can change the color and thickness of the individual sides. To add a border, first click an object you want. Then continue as follows:

To delete a border entirely, first click the object whose border you want to delete. Next, click the Line/ Border Style button on the Formatting toolbar. Finally, click the No Line command on the drop-down menu list.

Publisher applies a border inside a box frame. Therefore, avoid making the thickness of a border too wide. If a border is too wide, graphic objects may become compressed or some text in a text frame may become hidden.

To change an individual side of a border, after Step 3, click the side you want here. Then optionally perform Steps 4, 5 and 7.

To create a border that is made up of pictures on a text box, picture frame or rectangle, click the BorderArt button in the dialog box opposite, and choose your options.

1 On the Formatting toolbar, click the Line/ Border Style button.

2 You can quickly apply a border simply by clicking the desired line on the floating menu.

3 Alternatively, you can see more borders by clicking the More Lines command, to display the Format <object name>, dialog box.

4 Click a line thickness, or type a value in Weight.

5 (Optional) Click another color from the drop-down list.

6 Or, under Presets, click the Box button.

7 Click OK

Making objects opaque or transparent

In Publisher, all objects you create – including frames – have a default white fill color. Usually, the initial state is set to transparent. To make an object opaque, select it, and then press Ctrl+T.

  You can change several objects in a single action, by holding down Shift while you click each object you want to make transparent. Alternatively, draw a selection box around all the objects you want to change to select the entire group, then apply the steps on this page.

 If the apply transparent/ opaque operation does not appear to work, you may be trying to work on a non-compatible image imported from another application. The action works only with objects which originate in Publisher.

To change back to the original settings, press Ctrl+T again. You can build up a design that is perhaps made up of several individually drawn elements containing various fill colors, tints and pattern styles. You can further enhance a design by making some objects transparent.

If your document may be used as part of a website, think carefully about applying a pattern or gradient fill to a text frame. When you publish to the Web, Publisher converts this type of text frame to a graphic, and so will take longer for users to download.

When you make an object opaque, naturally, you won't see what is covered by the opaque object, unless you make it transparent again. If your picture is compatible but does not have a transparent portion, try using Publisher. Here's how. Click the picture you want, on the Picture toolbar click Set Transparent Color, then click the color on the picture you want to make transparent.

Working with shadows

Shadows can enhance the illusion of depth and can transform a plain shape into something entirely more striking. You can apply a shadow to any shape created with the drawing tools or around frames. To add further specialist shadowed effects to text, you can use the WordArt program that comes with Publisher.

To apply a simple shadow to an object, first, select the object you want. Next, on the Formatting toolbar, click Shadow Style, then click the style you want from the list of icons.

In the list of icons, you can also gain access to several other shadow settings. For example, to change the distance between a shadow and its source, click Shadow Settings, then click the Nudge button you want. To change the color of a shadow, click the down-arrow button next to the Shadow Color button, and click a new color. To make a shadow appear see-through, click Semitransparent Shadow. To remove a shadow, click No Shadow.

The boundaries and guides included in your publication never appear in print. To view your publication without the boundaries and guides shown, simply open the View menu and click Boundaries and Guides to remove the tick mark next to the command.

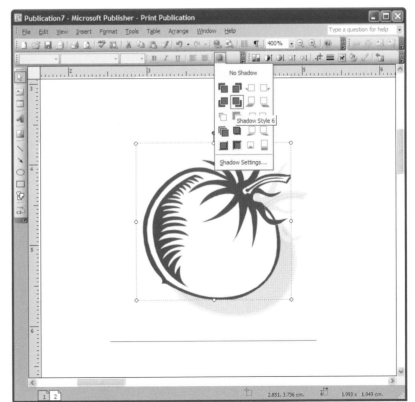

Drawing simple shapes

To draw a rectangle

Click the Rectangle tool near the lower part of the Objects toolbar. Place the mouse pointer where you want the top left-hand corner to start, then drag down diagonally towards the right. When you see the box shape you want, release the mouse button.

Using the Rectangle or Oval tool, to draw a precise square or circle, hold down the Shift key as you drag the mouse diagonally. To draw a rectangle or circle from the center outwards, hold down the Ctrl key as you drag the mouse diagonally. To draw a precise square or circle, from the center outwards, hold down both the Shift and Ctrl keys as you drag the mouse diagonally.

To draw a perfect square, see the tip in the margin. To draw a rectangle with a fancy border, first right-click inside the existing box. Next, from the floating menu, click Format AutoShape, then on the Colors and Lines tab, click the BorderArt button, make your choices and click OK as many times as you need to finish.

To draw an oval

First, click the Oval tool on the Objects toolbar, then drag an oval in a similar manner as described above, for a rectangle. To draw a perfect circle, see the first margin tip.

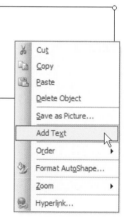

To change a freeform shape or curve

In the AutoShapes > Lines menu, you can access the Freeform and Curve tools. To change the shape of a freeform object or curve, first select the object you want. Next, open the Arrange menu and click Edit Points.

Any shape you create with the drawing tools is an object. So, you can change the size and proportion of a shape you draw by dragging the selection handles, as described on page 25.

You can then drag to reshape the shape or curve. To add a new shape point, click where you want to add, then drag. To delete a shape point, press Ctrl and click the shape point you want.

To draw an AutoShape

Publisher provides a collection of popular pre-created shapes, including rectangles, circles, stars, banners, callouts, arrows and connectors. To see the entire range of AutoShapes, first click the AutoShapes tool on the Objects toolbar. Next, click the shape category you want, followed by the exact shape you want. Also, see the margin tip to constrain any AutoShape you draw.

By using the Measurements toolbar, you can create and position objects precisely. To display it, using the right mouse button, click on any empty space on the Desktop and choose the Toolbars command, followed by the Measurements command.

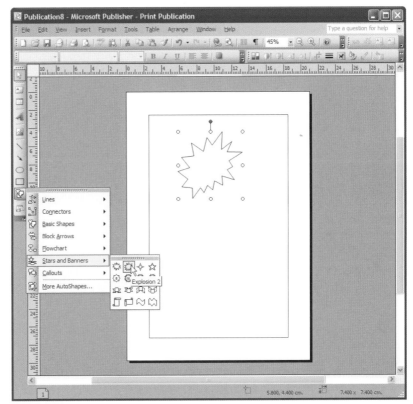

To resize any drawn shape

First, right-click the shape you want to resize. Then, from the floating menu, click Format <object type> command. In the Format <object type> dialog box, click the Size tab. In the Size and rotate section, and optionally in the Scale section, make your changes and click OK.

Working with lines and arrows

Lines can help give emphasis to, and separate, information within a document. In Publisher you can choose from a range of line styles and types, from plain lines and arrowhead lines to fancy lines – made up of individual elements using the BorderArt dialog box.

To give depth to a line, first click the line, then on the Formatting toolbar, choose from the options available in Line/Border Style button, Shadow Style button, or 3-D Style button.

To draw a simple line, perform the steps below:

1 Click the Line tool on the Objects toolbar.

2 Place your mouse pointer where you want your line to start, then drag your mouse to create the desired line length and angle you want.

To draw a straight line precisely, hold down the Shift key while you draw the line. Or press the Ctrl key to draw a straight line precisely from the center outwards.

3 (Optional) If you want to convert the line to an arrow, click the desired Arrow button on the Formatting toolbar.

4 (Optional) If you want to choose a different line style or see further arrow options, click the right mouse button over a selected line. Next, from the floating menu, click Format AutoShape, followed by the Colors and Lines tab. Click the line and arrow styles you want and click OK.

To create a fancy line, first draw a narrow box with the Box tool. Then click the Line/Border Style button on the Formatting toolbar, followed by the More Lines command. Click the BorderArt tab and choose your border. Click OK to finish.

To draw an arrow

You can draw an arrow from scratch simply by choosing the Arrow tool on the Objects toolbar, and following similar steps to those shown above for drawing a line.

To change the direction of a drawn arrow, first click the arrow you want. Then click the Rotate button you want on the Standard toolbar.

Drawing a 3D shape

To add or delete a 3-D effect from a drawn shape

First, click the shape you want to change. Next, on the Formatting toolbar, click 3-D Style. Then, from the drop-down panel that appears, click the effect you want.

In Publisher, you can apply a variety of special effects to text and objects, including 3-D, shadowing and embossing. You can add a shadow or emboss text onto an unfilled object containing text, or you can apply lots of related options from WordArt.

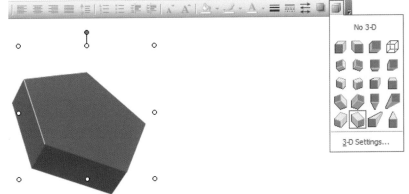

You can easily apply the same effect to several 3-D shapes at the same time. Here's how: simply select all the objects you want to change, before choosing the 3-D effect you want.

To see a wider range of 3-D effects

With the shape or object still selected, click 3-D Settings from the drop-down panel of icons and commands. Then click the options you want from the 3-D Settings toolbar shown below.

To delete a 3-D effect

Click the shape or object from which you want to remove the currently applied 3-D effect. Next, on the Formatting toolbar, click 3-D Style. Then click No 3-D at the top of the drop-down panel.

You can apply a shadow or a 3-D effect, not both. If you add a 3-D effect to an object that already has a shadow applied, Publisher deletes the shadow, and vice versa.

Changing the fill color or pattern

Publisher is rich in options that enable you to apply a range of different fills to a shape. Every shape you draw is given a default fill color and pattern. You can change colors, choose from a variety of patterns, or change both the color and the pattern.

To change the fill color or pattern, first right-click the object or shape you want. Then, from the floating menu, click the Format <object type> command. Click the options you want. You can choose either or both colors and fill effects, to change or apply a texture, pattern or gradient fill. See the example selections below.

If you're using more than one color, try to choose all of your colors from a single row in the Colors dialog box. The colors in each of the 12 rows have been arranged and chosen to work well together in a multi-color publication.

You can also get easy access to the Fill Color button and Fill Effects commands, by using the Formatting toolbar, providing you select an object or shape first.

If you plan to use graduated fills in your publication, it's a good idea to make some test prints as soon as possible. Some printers can't handle some graduated fills and patterns easily, and therefore may substitute a chosen color with a solid color, or even black.

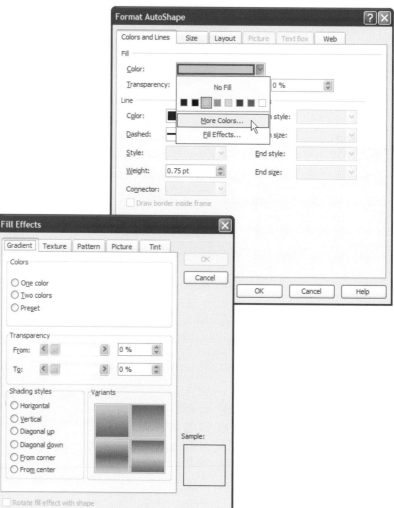

Using object linking and embedding

Objects can be created in other programs and included in a Publisher document. For example, you might want to use a chart created in Microsoft Excel. Furthermore, a linked object maintains a link to its original source program.

To view a list of all the programs on your system that are OLE-compatible, open the Insert menu and click the Object command. Then, use the scroll bar to view the contents of the Object Type box.

Often, the information used to form these objects may change, and so you need a method to make sure these objects can be updated easily, even if already placed in a Publisher document. The answer is provided by an enhancement called Object Linking and Embedding (OLE), which may be included in the software.

OLE ensures that if any such objects are placed within a Publisher document, you can start up the source program from within Publisher to edit the object using the tools from the source program – without leaving Publisher. For this to work however, you must first link or embed the desired object in a Publisher document, and also, the source program must be OLE-compatible.

Embed an object when you're the only person working on the publication, so that any changes you make to the contents of an embedded object affect only that publication.

Linking or embedding an object

To link or embed an object, first make sure no other object is selected in Publisher. Then carry out the steps below:

1 Open the Insert menu and click the Object command.

2 Click Create from File.

3 To embed an object, go straight to step 4. To link an object, click here first.

4 Click Browse.

Insert Object

- ☐ Create New
- ● Create from File

File: C:\Documents and Settings\Brian Austin

Browse... ☑ Link

☐ Display As Icon

OK
Cancel

Result: Inserts a picture of the file contents into your document. The picture will be linked to the file so that changes to the file will be reflected in your document.

Link an object if you're sharing a publication with other people or other documents. Then, any changes made to the content of an object in your publication can be reflected wherever that object exists.

5 In the Browse dialog box, navigate through the folders to find the file you want to link/embed, and click that file to select it. Click the Open button.

6 Click OK.

After Publisher has created the new linked or embedded object, you can move and resize the object as described earlier in this chapter.

Updating a linked object

To update the link to an object in your publication, first open the Edit menu and click Links. Then carry out the steps below:

1 In the list of linked objects, click the object you want to update.

4 Click Close or Cancel.

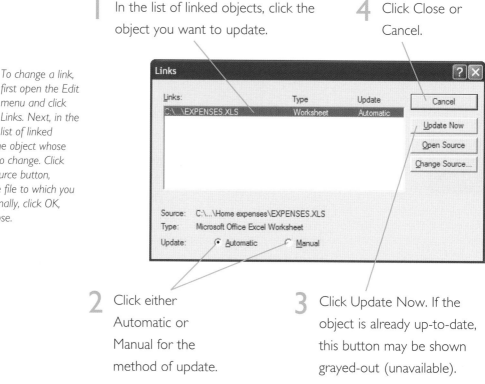

To change a link, first open the Edit menu and click Links. Next, in the list of linked objects, click the object whose link you want to change. Click the Change Source button, followed by the file to which you want to link. Finally, click OK, followed by Close.

2 Click either Automatic or Manual for the method of update.

3 Click Update Now. If the object is already up-to-date, this button may be shown grayed-out (unavailable).

Editing a linked or embedded object

To edit a linked or embedded object, first double-click the desired object. Next, make your changes using the source program's tools. To return to Publisher, click the Exit or Exit and Return command in the source program's File menu, followed by clicking Yes if prompted to save. However, if you can only see the Publisher Title bar, simply click outside the object workspace to return to Publisher proper.

Designing with text

As we might expect, text options and commands in Publisher are powerful, flexible and yet simple to apply. In this chapter, we discover how text is more than just words, and how to tap into powerful design aids, tools and options within Publisher.

Covers

Chapter Three

Entering text into Publisher

You can bring text into Publisher in the following ways:

- type directly into a text box frame

- copy text from another program or file

- import an entire text file from another program

- import direct from some versions of Microsoft Word

- link or embed text using Object Linking and Embedding

For now let's assume you draw a text frame at the size and location you want. Here's how. On the Objects toolbar, first click Text Box.

Next, in your publication, place the mouse pointer to one corner of where you want your text box to appear, then drag diagonally, until you have created the size and shape of text box you want. Now, you can start typing your text directly into the new text box.

The Text in Overflow symbol (**A ···**) appears when there's more text in a frame than can currently be viewed. To flow the remaining hidden text, first draw another text frame.

2 Click the Create Text Box Link button on the Standard toolbar.

3 The mouse pointer then changes into a pitcher symbol. Click in the text frame where you want to place the excess text from the first text frame.

4 Publisher "pours" the remaining text into the second frame; it places a Go To Next Text Box button at the bottom of the first text frame and a Go To Previous Text Box button at the top of this frame. Note: the Go To ... buttons are only visible in the text box frame containing the text cursor.

Once text has been flowed into multiple frames, you can easily follow the flow from one frame to the next simply by clicking the Go To Next Text Box ( ) and Go To Previous Text Box ( ) buttons.

With multiple connected text frames, if you want to disconnect a text frame from others in a sequence, first click in any connected text frame (other than the last in the list), then choose the Break Forward Link button on the Standard toolbar.

To import text, you can choose the Text File command on the Insert menu. Publisher can accept text saved in a variety of common word-processor formats, including Microsoft Word, WordPerfect and Rich Text Format (RTF).

Changing the basic look of text

To quickly highlight all text in a text box, click inside the text box you want, and press Ctrl+A. This is the keyboard shortcut for the Select All command in the Edit menu.

Changing a font

A font is a set of specific characters in a single typeface containing upper and lower case characters, punctuation marks and digits. Publisher comes with a wide range of different fonts and font styles. You can change the current font easily. First, highlight and select the text you want to change. Then, choose the new font you want from the drop-down list in the Font box on the Formatting toolbar.

Or, highlight the text you want to change, right-click and choose Change Text, followed by Font (or the command you want). The options shown in the Font dialog box are shown below:

If the amount of text is too large to fit in a text frame box, you have three options. You can: (1) reflow the text to another text box, or (2) enlarge an existing text box, or, (3) reduce the text size.

Click here if you want to choose another font.

Click here to underline text.

Click here if you want to change the text style: Regular, Italic, Bold, or Bold Italic.

Click here if you want to change the text size.

Sometimes, you may want to export text you create in Publisher, and continue to work on your document in another program. Publisher can save files in a range of different formats. If you're not sure which application you'll be using, then save the file in RTF format.

Click here if you want to change the text color

Click the appropriate check box to place a tick mark in each of the options you want here

Click here to make your changes

Click here to cancel your changes

A sample here shows how your changes will look

Other powerful text look and feel options

Remember, in the task pane, you also have direct access to two powerful command groups in Publisher: the Styles and Formatting pane and the Font Schemes pane.

Changing text alignment

Publisher provides four ways to align text: Align Left (the default), Align Right, Center and Justify. Align Left ensures that all lines in a text block align at the left margin. If you're creating lots of text, arguably, your readers find text easiest to read when aligned with Align Left (like this book).

Align Right aligns at the right margin to give a ragged left edge. Although normal readability can be affected, Align Right provides a refreshing contrast if used sparingly and in a considered way. For example, letterheads containing names and addresses, company logos, pull quotes, and so on, can provide a distinctive and stylish look when aligned at the right edge.

Center aligns each text line equally between the margins. Center alignment is ideal for headings, invitations and announcements. Justify spaces each text line equally between the margins and can provide a noticeable level of neatness and order, providing line width is wide and the font size reasonably small.

To change text alignment, perform the following steps:

To quickly clear all formatting previously applied to a text block, first highlight the text you want, display the Styles and Formatting task pane, then click the Clear Formatting command.

To change the alignment of an entire block of text, select the entire block before choosing the new text alignment button you want.

To align text vertically in a text box, first click the desired text box. Then, in the Format menu, choose Text Box, followed by the Text Box tab, and choose the option you want in the Vertical alignment category.

Justified text alignment applied to short text lines or lines containing large fonts can cause gap patterns or "rivers" of unsightly white space running down the page. Solution: use smaller font sizes and longer lines of text.

1 Click in the text box containing the text you want to change (also see the margin tips).

2 Click the button on the Formatting toolbar shown below, representing the alignment you want.

Align Left   Center   Align Right   Justify

Deleting text

You can delete specific text or an entire text box. Or, you may want to delete text inside a text box but not delete the text box itself. The following procedures describe your options when deleting text.

If you accidentally delete text you want to keep, before performing any other action, click the Undo button on the Standard toolbar, or choose the Undo command in the Edit menu.

To delete a single character at a time, click where you want to delete. Then, each time you want to delete one character to the left of the insertion point, press the Backspace key. Or, each time you want to delete one character to the right of the insertion point, press the Delete key.

Take extra care when deleting text. When you need to click in a text box, make sure that you click inside the box, not near the box edge. Selecting a text box instead of selecting all text in a text box, can result in deleting text you may want to keep.

Inside·Story·Headline

The following text consists of a mock Latin which has been based upon the average frequency of characters and word lengths of the English language in order to reproduce a reasonably accurate overall visual impression. Lorem ipsum dolor sit amet, consectetur adipscing elit, sed diam nonnumy eiusmod tempor incidunt ut labore et dolore magna aliquam erat volupat.¶

Et harumd dereud facilis est er expedit distinct. Nam liber

a tempor cum soluta nobis eligend optio comque nihil quod a impedit anim id quod maxim placeat facer possim omnis es voluptas assumenda est, omnis dolor repellend. Temporem autem quinsud et aur office debit aut tum rel cum necesit atib saepe eveniet ut er repudiand sint et molestia non este recusand.¶

The following text consists of a mock Latin which has been based upon the average frequency of characters and word lengths of the English

language in order to reproduce a reasonably accurate overall visual impression. Lorem ipsum dolor sit amet, consectetur adipscing elit, sed diam nonnumy eiusmod tempor incidunt ut labore et dolore magna aliquam erat volupat.¶

¶

Et harumd dereud facilis est er expedit distinct. Nam liber a tempor cum soluta nobis eligend optio comque nihil quod a impedit anim id quod maxim placeat facer possim

To delete some but not all text in a frame

1 Highlight the text you want to delete.

2 Press the Delete key.

To delete an entire text box and the text inside

1 Right-click inside the text box you want to delete.

2 From the floating menu, click the Delete Object command.

To delete all text in a chain of connected text boxes without deleting the text boxes

1 Click inside one of the text frames in the connected sequence (story).

2 Press Ctrl+A (the shortcut to highlight all text in the chain).

3 Press the Delete key.

Finding and replacing text

Finding text

You can use Publisher's Find command to quickly search for text containing specified characters in the selected text box. By default, Publisher flags all text containing the characters you specify. For example, if you enter the characters "ate", Publisher will flag "create", "date" and "ate" if these words are present in the text. However, you can tell Publisher to find only exact specific text, if you wish, and limit the search criteria by specifying whether to flag only uppercase or lowercase characters.

To delete all instances of the text that you're searching for, simply leave the Replace with edit box blank and click the Replace All button.

To find text, open the Edit menu and click Find. In the Find what box, type the text you want to find (if you want to search special characters, like end-of-paragraph markers, see Publisher Help to view the precise codes to enter). Next, choose any additional traits you want under Find options, then click Find Next.

To find and replace text

If the selected Text box is part of a series of connected frames, Publisher performs the search and replace action in all text boxes that make up the connected chain.

First, open the Edit menu and click Replace. In the Find and Replace dialog box, type in the Find what box, the text you want to find. Use a question mark for each character you're unsure of.

In the Replace with box, type the text you want to replace the found text with. Under Find options, select any additional options you want.

To have Publisher replace all instances of the target text in a single action, click the Replace All button. However, remember that with this option, you do lose control of individual actions, so be sure that this is really what you want to do.

Next, click Find Next, to have Publisher find the first instance of the text you're searching for. Then, click Replace, Replace All, or Find Next again, to continue the search and replace sequence. Repeat the steps in this paragraph as many time as necessary to finish.

Changing character spacing

Publisher provides you with the option to alter the spacing between characters – also known as tracking. This option can be useful if you want to improve the general look of text or to ensure specific text fits in the available space in a text box. For example, sometimes, the look of headlines made up of larger font sizes can be improved by reducing their character spacing.

Here's the difference between tracking and kerning. Tracking adjusts the space between characters in a block of text; kerning adjusts the space between certain pairs of characters only.

To change character spacing in a specific paragraph, first highlight the desired paragraph, or highlight all the paragraphs you want to change. Next, open the Format menu and click Character Spacing. Under tracking, choose the options you want – watch the preview window to get an idea of the effect. Click Apply to try out your choice. If satisfied, click OK, otherwise, click Cancel.

Changing character-pair kerning

What is kerning? Answer: the action of changing the spacing between certain pairs of characters that the human eye would otherwise perceive to be too close together or too far apart. The kerning values used vary from font to font.

Tight spacing brings letters closer together (condense); loose spacing moves letters further apart (expand).

Publisher ——— Normal spacing

Publisher ——— Tighter than normal spacing (condense)

Publisher ——— Looser than normal spacing (expand)

When you change character spacing, Publisher makes a "best guess." Sometimes, characters may overlap. If this happens, click a looser spacing option in the Character Spacing dialog box.

To change the default kerning, first highlight pairs of specific letters, or the words you want to change. Next, open the Format menu and click Character Spacing. Then, in the Character Spacing dialog box, under Kerning, click Expand or Condense. Choose the value you want in the By this amount box and click OK.

To change line and paragraph spacing

First, click in the paragraph you want to change, or select all the text you want to affect. Next, open the Format menu and choose the Paragraph command. You can then make your changes in the relevant sections in the dialog box that Publisher displays.

Changing text frame margins

When you draw a text box, Publisher applies default text margins within the text box you draw. For most purposes, these default settings may be adequate.

Sometimes however, you may want to change the margins. The following procedure shows you how to alter the size of the text frame margins.

You don't have to enter value for all four sides. You can enter a margin value for each side individually: Left, Right, Top or Bottom.

If you make the margins too wide, some of your text may seem to disappear. However, the excess text may only have flowed into the hidden overflow area under the text box frame. If that happens, expand your text frame, or create a new text frame and flow the excess text into it.

1 With the right mouse button, first, click in the text box you want to change.

2 Then, from the floating menu, click Format Text Box.

3 Next, click the Text Box tab.

4 Under the Text Box Margins section, click or type the values you want for the Left, Right, Top and Bottom margins.

5 Click OK to apply your new margin settings.

Creating a bulleted or numbered list

When you want to present information in a clear but loose tabular form, often a bulleted or numbered list is an ideal answer.

To quickly create or un-create, a bulleted list, first type your text line, then immediately click the Bullets or Numbering button on the Formatting toolbar. To remove the bullet or number, click the Bullets or Numbering button again. Continue working on each entry in your list as above.

Creating a bulleted list

To create a simple bulleted list, first click where you want to start the list to display an insertion point. If you want to convert existing text to a bulleted list, highlight the text you want to convert first. Finally, click Bullets on the Formatting toolbar. Then, each time you want to start a new line in your bullet list, press Enter. Also, see margin tip.

To create a customized bulleted list

First, highlight the text you want as described in the previous paragraph. Next, open the Format menu and click Bullets and Numbering. Under Bullet character, click the bullet type you want, or, to see more characters, click the Character button. Then, click the bullet character you want, followed by OK. Back in the Bullets and Numbering dialog box, optionally change the bullet size and indent distance. Click OK to finish.

While creating a bulleted or numbered list, to insert a new line without inserting a bullet or number, press Shift+Enter. To finish entering entries for your bulleted or numbered list, press Enter twice.

To remove bullets from a list

First highlight the bulleted list you want. Next, click the right mouse button over the highlighted list and choose Change Text, followed by Bullets and Numbering. Under the Bullet Character, click the first option (no bullets), followed by OK.

To remove numbering from a list, first highlight the list. Next, click the right mouse button over the highlighted list and choose Change Text followed by Bullets and Numbering. Under Format, select None, then click OK.

To create a numbered list

Numbered lists provide similar benefits to bulleted lists, except that a numbered list implies a series of steps in a procedure, a sequence of events, or a hierarchy of priorities. You can create a numbered list, using a similar procedure to creating a bulleted list, except click the Numbering button on the Formatting toolbar instead of Bullets. Editing is similar to editing bullets, except you click the Numbering tab in the Bullets and Numbering dialog box, choose your new options and click OK to apply your new choices.

Working with tab stops

Tab stops can help you accurately align text vertically at specific positions in a text box – particularly useful if working with tables. Use tab stops or indents rather than the Spacebar.

If you prefer, you can insert, edit and delete tabs singly or in multiples, by using the Tabs command in the Format menu to display the Tabs dialog box.

| On the ruler, click where you want tab stops to appear. Publisher indicates tabs with a marker (example above uses left tab alignment).

2 Click in first line of text. Press Tab to move text to the custom tab stop.

3 Repeat Step 2 on the following text line. Continue, until all your text is aligned at the new custom tab stop position.

To change tab alignment

Publisher offers four tab alignment options: left edge, right edge, center and decimal point. To change the alignment of highlighted text, first double-click the Tab you want on the horizontal rule. Then in the Tabs dialog box, under Alignment, choose the alignment you want and click OK.

To change the status of tab stops and leaders, you must highlight the text you want to affect, before choosing a command or starting a procedure.

To move or delete a tab stop

First, highlight the text you want to change. Then on the horizontal ruler, drag the tab marker you want to a new position, or off the ruler completely, to delete the tab.

To add and delete leaders to tab stops

Leaders – dots, dashes, or lines – combined with tab stops, can help guide the eye. Highlight the text you want. Double-click a tab stop marker on the ruler. In the Tabs dialog box, under Leader, click the leader you want. Then click OK. To delete leaders, highlight the text you want to affect, display the Tabs dialog box again, and click None under Leaders. Click OK to confirm your changes.

When you highlight text to change existing tabs, if you can't see the markers on the ruler, make sure that you've highlighted only the relevant text. If you highlight an area of text which does not have any tab formatting applied, Publisher may not display any tab markers on the ruler.

To delete all tab stops at the same time

First, highlight the text you want to affect. Then, in the Tabs dialog box, click the Clear All button, followed by the OK button.

Indenting text

When you insert a text indent you affect an entire paragraph, or more if you have highlighted multiple paragraphs.

To quickly delete indents in a highlighted paragraph, use the Decrease Indent button on the Formatting toolbar.

To quickly indent highlighted text, simply click the Increase Indent button on the Formatting toolbar.

To quickly adjust an indent, first highlight the text containing the indent you want to change. Then, on the ruler, place the mouse pointer on the desired indent marker and simply drag it to the new position.

Paragraph

Indents and Spacing | Line and Paragraph Breaks

General

Alignment: Left

Indentation

Preset: Hanging Indent   Left: 1cm

First line: -1cm   Right: 0cm

Line spacing

Before paragraphs: 0pt   Between lines: 1sp

After paragraphs: 0pt

☐ Align text to baseline guides

Sample

[OK] [Cancel] [Help]

To create an indent

First, highlight the paragraphs you want to indent. Next, open the Format menu, click Paragraphs, followed by the Indents and Spacings tab. Then, under Indentation, you can make your choices in the dialog box as shown above.

To create a specific type of indent, in the Preset drop-down list, you can choose between: Flush Left, 1st Line Indent, Hanging Indent, Quotation and Custom. If you choose Custom, you can set the values you want in the Left, Right and First line boxes.

To remove an indent

Display the Paragraph dialog box, as described in "To create an indent." Then, under Indentation, in the Preset list, click Flush left.

Working with text styles

A text style includes formatting attributes that you may apply to any paragraph, and can include font, type size, type style (i.e. whether bold, italic, or normal), line spacing, paragraph alignment, tabs, and indents.

While working on serial publications like newsletters, you could make the job much easier by defining separate individual styles for the headline, main headings, subheadings, body text, captions and so on, before you start creating your publication.

To create a new style and perform other key actions, first open the Format menu and click the Styles and Formatting command. In the Styles and Formatting task pane, you can create, change, rename, delete and import text styles.

Once you've defined a style, you can easily apply your new style to any paragraph in the current document in a single step. To define a new style, apply any of the style formatting attributes listed in the previous paragraphs, to reformat the text the way you want. Then, highlight the newly formatted text and perform the following steps:

Text styles are particularly useful when you're working on longer publications or documents that are part of a matched set. Using styles in this way, you can keep a consistent look to all related publications from different authors.

1 Click in the Style box on the Formatting toolbar and type a name for the new style.

2 Press Enter.

3 In the Create Style By Example dialog box, confirm that the style name, font name and size are correct, then click OK.

To apply a text style to a paragraph

First click in the paragraph you want. Then, in the Style box on the Formatting toolbar, click the drop-down arrow and click the style you want. The drop-down arrow button also provides access to the additional commands outlined above.

Defining a text style is only the first stage of the process. To use a defined text style, you must apply the style to a paragraph.

Create Style By Example

Enter new style name: Cool2

Sample

Verdana

Verdana 10

Description

Cool +

OK   Cancel

Using personal information sets

When you start a new publication, Publisher automatically selects the Primary Business Personal Information Set. However, you can choose which set – if any – you want to use for the current publication using the Personal Information command in the Edit menu.

Often, the same information can be used repeatedly throughout various publications. Publisher makes the job of handling repeated personal information easier by providing personal information sets. A personal information set contains basic essential information about you, your business or organization. A group of related components make up a personal information set. Each personal information set contains the following components: personal name, job title, name of organization, address of organization, organization's tag line, telephone, fax and e-mail numbers, organization's logo, color scheme.

With a personal information set, you need only enter this information once. From then on, you can choose to use the information in its native form, or modify it "on the fly".

To create and update personal information data

Open the Edit menu and click the Personal Information command. Choose which personal information set you want: Primary business (default), Secondary business, Other organization, or Home/family. Then enter or edit your information in the dialog box below, and click Update to finish. You can then apply a component to a publication, using the Personal Information command in the Insert menu.

To change information in a personal information set, first make your changes as described on this page. Finally, save your publication.

If you make a change to one instance of a personal information component in a publication, Publisher also changes all other instances of the same type of component to match.

Personal Information

Click Update to save your changes and update this personal information set in your publication.

Select a personal information set:

Primary Business

Personal information for this set

My name:

Brian Austin

Job or position title:

Author, Web Designer

Organization name:

Business Name

Address:

Primary Business Address
Your Address Line 2
Your Address Line 3
Your Address Line 4

Phone, fax, and e-mail:

Phone: 555-555-5555
Fax: 555-555-5555
E-mail: someone @example.com

Tag line or motto:

Your business tag line here.

☐ Include color scheme in this set

Select a color scheme:

Citrus

Logo

Update   Cancel   Help

Getting creative with WordArt

WordArt is without doubt, one of Publisher's most amazing text design assistants. The power, design options and choices are awesome! Use the Insert WordArt tool, on the Objects toolbar, to create a range of special graphic effects to words, like the example shown below. To start WordArt, carry out the steps below:

1   Click the Insert WordArt tool on the Objects toolbar:

WordArt is great for trying out ideas and letting your imagination fly. You can twist and turn text, wrap words around a shape, apply patterns, colors and shadows, and much more.

2   Publisher displays the WordArt Gallery dialog box. Click the WordArt style you want.

If you decide to use WordArt, print the WordArt page to check that the result is what you expect. WordArt effects can make extra demands on some printers. Depending on the quality and type of printer you're using, sometimes text that may look fine on the screen, could appear too jagged when printed.

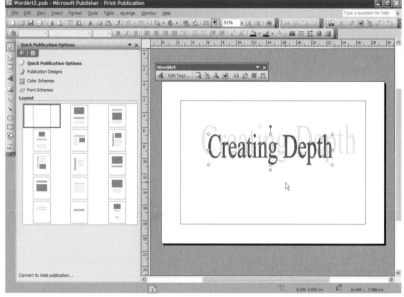

3   In the Edit WordArt Text dialog box that appears, type the text you want. Choose any other formatting options also available, if required. To start a new line, press Enter. Click OK.

4   Use the commands and buttons on the WordArt toolbar to apply various effects to your WordArt text.

5   Drag your WordArt box to box to the desired position on the page.

Creating a fancy first letter

If you want to add some pizazz to your publication, consider creating a stylish fancy first letter, or drop-cap.

Although usually, we may prefer to apply this effect to only the first letter in a text box, Publisher provides the means to apply the same technique to an entire word if you wish. To create a fancy first letter, carry out the steps below. See margin notes for additional options.

The following text consists of a mock Latin which has been based upon the average frequency of characters and word lengths of the English language in order to reproduce a reasonably accurate overall visual impression. Lorem ipsum dolor sit amet, consectetur adipscing elit, sed diam nonnumy eiusmod tempor incidunt ut labore et dolore magna aliquam erat volupat.

Et harumd dereud facilis est er expedit distinct. Nam liber a tempor cum soluta nobis eligend optio comque nihil quod a impedit anim id quod maxim placeat facer possim omnis es voluptas assumenda est, omnis dolor repellend. Temporem autem quinsud et aur office debit aut tum rerum necesit atib saepe eveniet ut er repudiand sint et molestia non este recusand.

To create a fancy first word, first count the number of letters in the word. Next, perform Steps 1 and 3 on this page. Then, click the Custom Drop Cap tab. In the Number Of Letters box type the number of letters in the first word. Finally, click OK.

1 With the right mouse button, click the paragraph into which you want to add a fancy first letter.

2 From the floating menu, click Change Text followed by the Drop Cap command.

3 In the Drop Cap dialog box, click the fancy letter you want. Use the scroll bar to see more letters. Click OK to finish.

To change or remove a fancy first letter, first click in the paragraph containing the letter. Next, click Change Drop Cap in the Format menu. To change the letter, click Custom Drop Cap and make your changes. To remove the letter, click the Remove button. Finally, click OK.

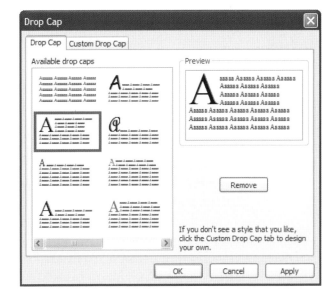

About Publisher's non-printing marks

Viewing or hiding Publisher's special characters

As you enter data into your document, Publisher inserts various non-printing special characters, as a design and layout aid while you work on your publication.

If the document in which you're working contains many varying text and graphic elements, it can be useful periodically to turn off special characters, boundaries and guides to see a clearer picture of your document.

Examples include paragraph marks – these appear every time you press Enter – tab marks, that Publisher inserts every time you press the Tab key, and space marks, that appear each time you press the Spacebar.

Publisher provides you with the commands to view or hide any non-printing characters. When non-printing characters are visible, if you want to hide them, simply open the View menu and click the Special Characters command.

When boundaries and guides are turned off, but the Snap > To Guides command in the Arrange menu is turned on, remember, the snapping action is still active when you move or place objects.

To display the special characters when they are hidden, simply click Special Characters in the View menu. In addition to the obvious differences in your publication (see the two illustrations above), next to the Special Characters command, Publisher indicates whether the command is currently on or off.

Viewing or hiding boundaries and guides

Publisher also lets you display or hide object boundaries and guides. To hide boundaries and guides when they are visible, simply open the View menu and click the Boundaries and Guides command. To display boundaries and guides, click the Boundaries and Guides command again.

Working with pictures

A carefully selected and prepared picture can add spice, life and panache to an otherwise lackluster publication. In this chapter, we explore this important topic and how to use Publisher's powerful range of picture options and commands.

Covers

Chapter Four

Placing a picture on the page

Bitmap pictures are made up of a series of aligned dots. Avoid stretching or enlarging a bitmap picture to prevent jagged appearance. Vector-based images however, can usually be scaled or stretched without loss of quality.

Pictures provide a focal point to a page that text can never quite equal. Publisher comes with thousands of pictures comprising clip art, photos and animations stored in the Clip Gallery. You can also download additional images from the Microsoft Office Web site (see Publisher Help). Although images come in a range of different file types, all images can be grouped into two categories: bitmapped or vector. Bitmapped pictures include clip art with filename extensions of .bmp, .jpg, .gif, and .tif, whereas common vector-based clip art filename extensions include, .eps, .wmf, and .cgm.

To place a picture on the page

To view the range of picture formats Publisher can import, click Picture in the Insert menu, followed by From File. Then click the Files of type arrow button.

On the Objects toolbar, first click the Picture Frame tool, followed by one of four commands: Clip Art, Picture from File, Empty Picture Frame, or From Scanner or Camera. If relevant, make any further choices. With the Picture crosshair mouse pointer, click on the page where you want to place your picture or picture frame (unless you're importing from a scanner or camera). Then, adjust the size and modify as you want.

To replace a picture with a different picture

You can move a picture using the Edit > Cut and Edit > Paste commands. Also, you may be able to move an object to another Windows application using the Paste command in your target Windows application.

Open the Tools menu and click Graphics Manager. In the Graphics Manager task pane, under the Select a picture list, click the down-arrow button next to the picture you want to change, then click Replace this Picture. In the Insert Picture dialog box, find the picture you want, then click it. Next, click the down-arrow button next to the Insert button. If you want to embed the picture, click Insert. If you want to insert the picture as a linked picture, click Link to File. You can learn more about linking and embedding on page 39.

Changing the screen redraw speed

To copy a picture, first, click the picture you want, then choose Copy from the Edit menu. Next, go to where you want to place a copy of the picture, and choose Paste from the Edit menu.

The size and complexity of a picture affects how quickly your PC draws its image on the screen. If images take too long to redraw when you zoom or move from page to page, you can speed up screen redraw, reduce the resolution or even hide the images entirely, leaving picture placeholders where your pictures would normally appear.

To change your picture display resolution, first open the View menu, click Pictures, click the option you want and then click OK to finish.

How to resize, crop or delete a picture

As you place text and graphic objects on your page, you can adjust the individual elements to achieve the desired balance. As a picture is an object, you can resize as it outlined in the steps on page 25.

To quickly make a copy or multiple copies of a picture, first press and hold down the Ctrl key, then drag the picture to where you want. When you release the mouse button, Publisher creates an identical copy at the new location. Repeat as many times as necessary.

To resize a picture with precision

First click the picture you want to change, then open the Format menu and click Picture. In the Format Picture dialog box, click the Size tab. Under Scale, select the Height and Width values you want, and any other desired Scale options, then click OK. To restore the original dimensions, display the Format Picture dialog box, and Size tab as above. Click Reset, followed by OK.

Cropping a picture

Sometimes, you may not want to use an entire picture in a publication, just a section. You can manipulate or hide parts of a picture using the Crop tool. When you

crop a picture, you're not actually deleting the part you crop. If you change your mind later, you can easily uncrop the picture to restore the original image.

Remember, you can resize several pictures at the same time by grouping the pictures you want to resize, as described on page 29.

To crop a picture, first click the picture you want, then on the Picture toolbar, click the Crop tool. Publisher places cropping handles around the selected picture. Place the Crop tool mouse pointer over a top, bottom, left, right, or corner cropping handle.

To crop one side of an image, drag the center cropping handle on the side you want. To crop both sides evenly at the same time, press and hold down Ctrl while you drag a center cropping handle. To crop all four sides evenly at the same time, press and hold down Ctrl while you drag a corner cropping handle. To finish, click the Crop tool again to turn off the crop command.

If you want to place a picture that isn't part of Publisher's Clip Gallery, on the Objects toolbar, click Picture Frame, followed by Picture from File and follow the remaining instructions.

To delete a picture from a page

First, right-click the picture you want, and then, from the floating menu, click Delete Object. Alternatively, after selecting the picture, press the Delete key.

Changing the colors in a picture

After you place a picture on the page, you may be able to change all the colors in the picture to different shades of a single color – though not Encapsulated PostScript (EPS) images.

To recolor a picture, first, right-click the picture you want. Next, from the floating menu, click the Format Picture command. Then complete the remaining steps below.

1 In the Format Picture dialog box, click the Recolor button.

3 Click the color you want.

2 In the Recolor dialog box, click the color down-arrow button, to display the colors palette.

Recolor Picture

Preview

○ Recolor whole picture
○ Leave black parts black

Color: [____] ▾

Restore Original Colors

OK   Cancel   Apply

4 (Optional) Click More Colors to see more choices.

6 (Optional) If desired, select Leave black parts black. Otherwise, let the default apply.

5 (Optional) Click Fill Effects to apply a tint or shade, then make your choices.

7 Click OK, twice.

Using the Clip Art task pane

Some benefits of using the Clip Art task pane

Publisher's Clip Art task pane can be a powerful aid to your desktop publishing. The task pane helps organize your clips and provides quick access to pictures from three key sources: (1) those stored on your PC that may come from various sources, (2) images that come with Publisher, and (3) thousands more quality images available from the Microsoft Office Online website.

To create a new category for your clip, in the Clip Organizer, open the File menu and click New Collection. Then, in the New Collection dialog box, type a new Collection name, select where to put your new category, then click OK.

To quickly display the Clip Art task pane

On the Objects toolbar, click the Picture Frame tool, followed by the Clip Art command.

Alternatively, open the Insert menu, click Picture, and then click Clip Art.

To place a picture from the Clip Art task pane onto the publication page

First, using the task pane down-arrows, various options, and the Go button, you can have Publisher search for the kinds of pictures you want.

Microsoft also provides access to tens of thousands items of clip art, photos, animations and sounds at Microsoft Office Online. Click the link Clip art on Office Online at the bottom of the Clip Art task pane, and connect to the Internet.

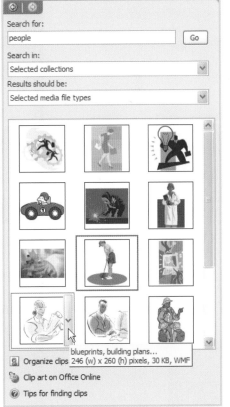

If you no longer want to keep specific images in the Clip Organizer, you can delete them. If you do this, remember you're not actually deleting them from your hard disk, only from the Organizer.

Then, once Publisher has identified the relevant images, to insert a picture, simply move your mouse pointer over the image icons, and click the icon representing the image you want. Or, click the down-arrow next to the icon image to access a range of further commands, like Insert, Copy, Delete and Preview.

To access more free Publisher images, click Clip art on Office Online. Publisher prompts you to connect to the Internet.

Organizing your clip art in Publisher

The Clip Organizer

Towards the bottom of the Clip Art task pane, you can view the Organize clips link. When you click Organize clips, Publisher opens a new window to display the Microsoft Clip Organizer, in which you can access clips stored in logical categories.

You can easily see the range of file formats which Publisher can import. In the Clip Organizer, open the File menu and click Add Clips to Organizer, followed by On My Own. Then, Just click the down-arrow button next to the Files of type box. Clips are categorized by type: Pictures, Photos, Sounds and Motion.

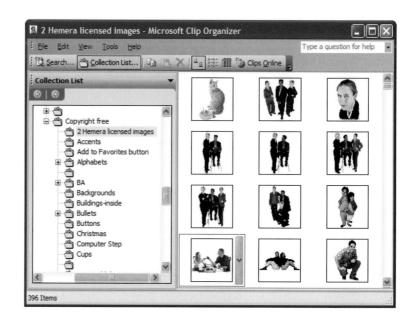

To delete a picture, click the down-arrow on the right side of the image you want, then choose the Delete command. To delete a collection of pictures that you have created, right-click on the collection name, then click the Delete command.

The Clip Organizer can store all your clip art in one place, and makes the job of finding, previewing and placing a picture on a page easy. Clip art created in other applications can also be stored in the Clip Organizer, including sound and video files. You can create new Categories and modify the descriptions of existing Categories.

To directly access an image in the Clip Organizer, move your mouse pointer over the images, click the drop-down arrow button next to the image you want, and click Copy. Back in your Publisher publication, click a blank picture frame. Right-click in the frame, and click Paste.

You can use the Search tool in the Clip Organizer to quickly locate the picture file you want to work with, or delete.

To add a picture to the Clip Organizer

In the Clip Organizer, open the File menu, and click Add Clips to Organizer, followed by the command you want: Automatically, On My Own, or From Scanner or Camera. Follow remaining steps.

Using mail merge and catalog merge

In this chapter, we explore mail merge and catalog merge, Publisher's amazingly powerful toolset, to help you combine information from two sources, and create customized mass-mailed publications like form letters, address labels, and so on.

Covers

Chapter Five

Introducing mail and catalog merge

Mail merge and catalog merge enable you to combine information from two sources, in such a way that you can create multiple customized publications more quickly than each publication could be created separately.

Example: imagine, you may want to send the same letter to 1,000 different people, yet make each letter appear customized to each individual recipient – name, address, salutation, and so on.

What's involved in a mail merge or catalog merge?

When you complete a mail merge, you'll do the following steps:

1 Choose a merge type: mail merge or catalog merge (guidelines for mail merge, start here; for catalog merge, see page 80).

2 Establish and choose a data source (see pages 65–69).

3 Design your merge publication and insert merge fields (for mail merge, see pages 74–78; for catalog merge, see pages 80–83 and page 84).

4 Preview your merge (for mail merge, see page 79; for catalog merge, see page 82).

5 Print your merge publication (page 84).

A closer look at Publisher mail merge

Mail merge combines two components: a list of information known as a data source and a conventional publication.

A data source can be a list of addresses or a series of pictures.

Within a mail merge publication, Publisher uses special merge fields that act as placeholders to represent the true information within the data source, to be merged later.

You can use Publisher mail merge in two key ways: (1) to automatically mass-mail lots of envelopes, letters, newsletters, brochures and other publications; (2) when you want to personalize many publications of the same type – perhaps add the recipient's first name.

In addition, pages that have been merged can be added to the end of an existing non-merged publication.

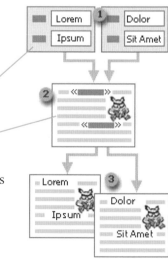

What's a data source and data field?

Data source

A data source is a list of information. For example, a data source can be a list of addresses or a series of pictures.

A data source list is actually made up of individual records, such as names, addresses, or even paths to images that you may use. To create a Publisher mail merge, you must use an existing, compatible data source.

Data field

A data field is a category that makes up a column of information within a data source.

Each data field you create, corresponds to an accompanying merge field that you'll place in your mail merge publication or catalog merge template.

The illustration below shows a data source with its relevant data fields. You can identify each data field by looking at the first row (header row) in the data source. The data fields used in a list of addresses might be called, for example: "Last Name", "First Name", etc.

Typical data source example: a list of addresses

Data fields shown in the header row

Remember, column names in a data source are used as corresponding merge field names, that you insert into a publication or catalog merge template.

Each complete row in a data source is a record (a set of related information about one item or entry).

Mail Merge Recipients

To sort the list, click the appropriate column heading. To narrow down the recipients displayed by a specific criteria, such as by city, click the arrow next to the column heading. Use the check boxes or buttons to add or remove recipients from the mail merge.

List of recipients:

	Last Name	First Name	Title	Company Name	Address Lin
☐	Smith	Jane	Miss	ACME Computing P...	555 Nice Road Wa
☑	Fliesgood	Phil	Mr	TR Byplane Wing-W...	Attitude House
☑	Austin	Brian	Mr	SoftRight Services	Address line 1

Select All   Clear All   Refresh

Find...   Edit...   Validate   OK

Setting up your data source

How to create a data source for a mail merge or catalog merge

Using a compatible external data source can save you time if your data source has many entries or if you regularly perform mail or catalog merges.

Before you can make use of Publisher's mail and catalog merge features, you'll need a mailing list of addresses or some other data source.

Your data source should contain all the individual records of information you want to apply to your mail merge publication. Your data source can also be created outside of Publisher, using a range of standard word-processor and database formats.

When you create/design your data source, make sure that it includes all the data fields you will need to perform your mail or catalog merge.

Examples include: those from Microsoft Word, Access, Excel, Outlook, SQL, dBASE, FoxPro and Oracle. Or, you can create your data source within Publisher as outlined below.

Mail and Catalog Merge ▾ ✕

Select a merge type

To work with records from a data source, do one of the following:

To add name and address information directly to your publication, select Mail Merge.

To create a new catalog merge template to use with multiple publications, select Catalog Merge.

◉ Mail Merge
○ Catalog Merge

Mail Merge

Create form letters, bulk mailings, or personalized publications.

Click Next to continue.

Step 1 of 5

➡ Next: Select data source

ⓦ Help with Mail and Catalog Merge

Creating your data source in Publisher

Remember to first consider what kinds of information you'll want in your data source. Some data sources have a simple structure. For example, if you want to create a simple list of addresses, the kinds of information items you'll most likely need are: first names, last names, street number, street name, city, state and zip code.

As well as making text entries, you can also merge pictures using an Address List. To do this, you'll need to add fields for each picture entry in your list, to represent and point to where the picture information is located. For more details, see page 77.

Each information item above is termed a data field, and will match the merge field that you place into your Publisher merge publication later. After you've created your data source in Publisher, save it for reuse later. Perform the steps below to create a data source comprising an address list:

Open the Tools menu, choose Mail and Catalog Merge, then click the Create Address List command.

Before entering the information for your address list, you can add additional fields to the list that display in the New Address List dialog box (see first margin tip on page 70).

In the New Address List dialog box, Publisher automatically saves the information for each new address when you click the New Entry button.

2 (Optional) Add any additional fields to the New Address List dialog box at this stage, before entering information for your address list.

3 Under the Enter Address information section, start typing the information for your first entry. When you've finished, click New Entry.

New Address List

Enter Address information

Title	Dr
First Name	John
Last Name	Makemewell
Company Name	
Address Line 1	
Address Line 2	
City	
State	

New Entry   Delete Entry   Find Entry...   Filter and Sort...   Customize...

View Entries

View Entry Number   First   Previous   1   Next   Last

Total entries in list   1

Close

4 Continue adding all entries as described in Step 3. Click Close when finished.

5 Publisher displays the Save Address List dialog box. In the File name box, type a name for your address list. Unless you save your address list to another location, when you click Save, Publisher saves your new data source in the My Data Sources folder.

6 Choose where you want to save your data source address list – ideally, keep to the default folder – then click Save.

How to create a data source for a mail merge or catalog merge that lists text and images using either Microsoft Excel or Microsoft Word

Whichever software you use, your source information is automatically arranged in table format. Information in the table columns provide the required data fields. The top row of your table is the header row in your data source and must list the column (data field) names. Perform the steps below:

After creating an address list data source, if you want to edit the list, click the Edit Address List command in the Tools > Mail and Catalog Merge menu. Then double-click on the list you want to edit.

To merge images, Publisher needs to know the name of each image, or have a path address to where each image is located (see margin tip below). An example name is: softright-logo.jpg. So, you'll need to either name the image or state the path to the image in Step 5.

Remember, a path is like a pointer to a location. Example: C:\Documents and Settings\Jane Smith\My Documents\My Pictures\softright-logo.jpg.

1 Microsoft Excel: create the worksheet that you want to use as your data source. Or, for Microsoft Word: create the table you want to use as a data source.

2 In the top left-hand cell, type a unique name for the column heading. For example, you may want to use labels like: Name, About, Image and so on.

3 Move to the cell immediately to the right and repeat Step 2 for that column. Continue until the header row contains names for each column in the table or worksheet.

4 With the top "header" row complete, move to next row down in the table and type each relevant snippet of information into each cell.

5 To merge images into a publication, either enter the name of the image or the path to the image you want (see second and third margin tips).

6 Repeat Steps 4 and 5 as many times as necessary to type all the entries.

7 On the File menu of Microsoft Word or Microsoft Excel, click the Save As command.

8 In the Save As dialog box, Move to the My Data Sources folder and open it. In the File name box, type a name that you want to use for your data source file. Click Save to finish.

Changing a data source

After you have set up a data source for a mail merge or catalog merge publication, you can still substitute the original data source with an alternative data source. Here's how.

You can apply a similar sort of procedure when working with a catalog merge.

Each column heading that you create becomes a merge field, which you can place in your mail merge publication or catalog merge template.

If you save your data source file in a location other than the My Data Sources folder, remember that when you come to open the data source for mail merge or catalog merge, you'll need to browse to the specific folder to locate your data source.

A database comprises a group of related information, e.g. employee records. Data in a database is organized into tables, records and fields. In Publisher, a table is a grid of rows and columns. A record is one row of cells.. A field is an individual cell within a row.

1 Open the mail merge publication or catalog merge template associated with the data source you want to change.

2 Open the Tools menu, choose Mail and Catalog Merge, then click Open Data Source.

3 Publisher asks if you want to connect to a different data source: click Yes.

4 When the Select Data Source dialog box displays, click the name of the new data source you want to use. If necessary, navigate to the location where the data source you want is stored.

5 Click the Open button or command. In the publication, Publisher replaces each original merge field name set up by the old data source, and inserts "<<missing merge field>>" instead. Now you can set up the merge fields normally as outlined on page 74.

Creating an address list

How to create an address list for a mail merge

First, identify and gather together in one place, the source material for the various kinds of information you want to include within your finished merge publication. For example, to create address labels, you'll need address information. Continue as follows:

You can add fields in the New Address List dialog box before you start entering information for your list. Here's how: 1. Click the Customize button. 2. Click Add in the Customize Address List dialog box. 3. In the Add Field dialog box, type a name for the new field you're creating. 4. Click OK. 5. Repeat Steps 2 and 3 to add any additional fields you want. 6 Click OK to finish.

1 Open the Tools menu and choose Mail and Catalog Merge, followed by the Create Address List command.

2 Publisher displays the first blank entry in the New Address List dialog box. Under Enter Address information, type the appropriate information into in each field.

3 When you've completed the entry, click the New Entry button.

An address list is a data source – a file of information that is merged with a conventional Publisher publication. Any merge must connect with a compatible data source in order to create the final merged publications.

New Address List

Enter Address information

Title	Dr
First Name	John
Last Name	Makemewell
Company Name	
Address Line 1	
Address Line 2	
City	
State	

New Entry | Delete Entry | Find Entry... | Filter and Sort... | Customize...

View Entries

View Entry Number | First | Previous | 1 | Next | Last

Total entries in list | 1

Close

In Step 6, by default, Publisher prompts to save to the My Data Sources folder. Ideally, keep to this location (however, you can choose another location if you prefer).

4 Repeat Steps 2 and 3 for each new additional entry you want to create.

5 Click Close when finished.

6 Publisher displays the Save Address List dialog box. In the File name box, type a name (see third margin Tip). Click Save

Filtering an address list

Sometimes, you may not want every record included in a mail merge. To merge only records or recipients that meet specific requirements, perform the following steps.

If you want to omit a particular record, click the check box to the left of the record you want to omit, to delete the tick from the check box.

To prepare for filtering

1 Open your mail merge publication. Display the Mail and Catalog Merge task pane.

2 Move the wizard on to Step 2: Select data source, and click Edit recipient list.

3 Now choose either the filter below or the one listed overleaf.

To filter using a single trait

If you want to narrow the list using a single trait (such as City), perform the steps below:

While you're experimenting with the powerful filtering options, if you change your mind, to display all records at any time: click (All).

1 Click the arrow in the specific column header you want to filter by. Now do either Step 2 and 3 to complete this filter sequence.

To filter using several conditions, the data source must: (1) contain records that have the same information, and (2) have ten or fewer unique values in the column you choose.

Before you can change the list of recipients, your mail merge publication must be connected to a data source.

Mail Merge Recipients

To sort the list, click the appropriate column heading. To narrow down the recipients displayed by a specific criteria, such as by city, click the arrow next to the column heading. Use the check boxes or buttons to add or remove recipients from the mail merge.

List of recipients:

	Last Name	First Name	Title	Company Name	Address Lin
☐	Smith	Jane	Miss	ACME Computing P…	555 Nice Road Wa
☑	Fliesgood	Phil	Mr	TR Byplane Wing-W…	Attitude House
☑	Austin	Brian	Mr	SoftRight Services	Address line 1

Select All   Clear All   Refresh
Find...   Edit...   Validate   OK

2 Click (Blanks) to display every record in which the current field is blank.

3 Click (Nonblanks) to display every record in which the current field contains any information.

To filter using several traits

Here's how:

Why use multiple filters? Answer: sometimes, you may want to filter using several conditions at the same time. For example, you may want to list all addresses listed within Texas, Germany or Colorado.

1. Click the arrow button in any column heading, then click (Advanced...). In the Filter and Sort dialog box, click the Filter Records tab.

2. In the Field box, choose the first field by which you want to filter. In the Comparison box, choose the phrase by which you want to compare the field you just chose. In the Compare box, type the specific text or series of numbers you want to compare with what you entered in the Field box.

Filtering does not affect the storage or accuracy of addresses in your data source, only how information is presented.

Mail Merge Recipients

To sort the list, click the appropriate column heading. To narrow down the recipients displayed by a specific criteria, such as by city, click the arrow next to the column heading. Use the check boxes or buttons to add or remove recipients from the mail merge.

List of recipients:

	Last Name	First Name	Title	Company Name	Address Lin
☑	Smith	(All)	iss	ACME Computing P...	555 Nice Road W
☑	Fliesgood	Jane	r	TR Byplane Wing-W...	Attitude House
☑	Austin	Phil	r	SoftRight Services	Address line 1
		Brian			
		(Blanks)			
		(Nonblanks)			
		(Advanced...)			

Select All   Clear All   Refresh

Find...   Edit...   Validate   OK

In Step 3, here's an imaginary And filter condition: when the last name is Pederson AND you want to mail merge to all Smiths who live in say, Florida.

3. If you want apply another filter to the one you created in Step 2, click the And option, and make the entries as outlined in Step 2. If you want to apply a filter that meets conditions for Step 2 or Step 3, click Or. To add additional filters, repeat Step 2 or Step 3.

4. When finished, click OK to register your choices in the Filter and Sort dialog box. Back in the Mail Merge Recipients dialog box, click OK again, to apply your new narrowed filter sequence.

Sorting an address list

By default, Publisher keeps to the original order in which you entered your address list data. However, you can change the order. For example, you may want to sort mailing labels to print in ascending postal code order. Or, you may want alphabetical order. To change the sort order, perform the steps below:

Sorting is possible only when you have merged (connected) your publication with a data source and inserted at least one placeholder within the publication.

1 Display Step 2: Select data source in the Mail and Catalog Merge task pane. Then click Edit recipient list.

2 To sort using a single trait, go to Step 3. To sort using multiple traits at the same time, go to Step 4.

Sorting an address list does not affect the essential information in any way. A sort simply rearranges the address order in one of two ways: ascending or descending order.

3 Click the column header you want. For example, if one of your headers is called City, click City to sort in ascending order. Click City again to sort in descending order. Click OK twice to finish.

Filter and Sort

Filter Records | Sort Records

Sort by: Last Name — ● Ascending ○ Descending

Then by: City — ● Ascending ○ Descending

Then by: — ● Ascending ○ Descending

Clear All   OK   Cancel

After re-sorting, to confirm the new sort order before printing, you can click the Show Merge Results command in the Tools > Mail and Catalog Merge menu. Then use the navigation buttons in the Mail and Catalog Merge pane to step through the addresses in your data source publication. If you need to zoom in to see entries more clearly, press F9.

4 Click a down-arrow button next to any column heading, then click Advanced. In the Filter and Sort dialog box, click the Sort Records tab. In the Sort by box, choose the first field by which you want to sort, then choose either Ascending or Descending order. Optionally, repeat this procedure in the first and second Then by boxes. Click OK. In the Mail Merge Recipients dialog box, also click OK.

Placing mail merge fields onto a page

You can format, move, copy and delete merge fields/placeholders in the same way as ordinary text.

A merge field is a name Publisher uses as a placeholder to represent the real text or images you want insert into a mail merge or catalog merge publication.

To insert merge fields, your mail merge publication or catalog merge template must first be connected to a data source.

If you use the Mail and Catalog Merge wizard to create your mail or catalog merge, Publisher prompts you to choose and insert your merge fields during Step 3.

You can also display the Insert Field dialog box/ pane, by clicking the Insert Field command in the Tools > Mail and Catalog Merge menu.

When you perform the actual merge later, Publisher takes the information that you set up earlier in your data source, inserts the real information from each data source record, and places it into each matching merge field in your publication, at the locations where the placeholders point.

When you choose to insert a merge field as text (the default), Publisher inserts the field at the insertion point in the selected text frame in your publication. If you choose Insert as Picture, Publisher places a merge field in a picture frame and inserts it at the insertion point you selected.

To insert merge fields, first open the publication you want, then perform the following steps:

Mail and Catalog Merge

Create your publication

If you have not already done so, create your publication now.

To add recipient information to your publication, click a location in the publication, and then click the item you want to insert below.

- Address block...
- Greeting line...
- Address fields...

Point to the field that you want to insert. When the drop-down arrow appears, click the arrow, and then click Insert as Text or Insert as Picture.

T	Title
T	First Name
T	Last Name
T	Company	Insert as Text
T	Address L	Insert as Picture
T	Address L
T	City
T	State
T	ZIP Code

Step 3 of 5

➡ Next: Preview your publication

⬅ Previous: Select data source

❔ Help with Mail and Catalog Merge

1 If you want to change the current data source, choose a new one (see page 69).

2 In your publication, click to place an insertion point at the location where you want to insert your first merge field. To zoom in quickly, press the F9 key.

...cont'd

Sometimes, data field names you use in your data source may not match the names of the fields Publisher uses. In these instances, click the Match Fields button and use the drop-down lists to match the fields as necessary.

3 Open the Tools menu, choose Mail and Catalog Merge, then choose the Insert Field command.

4 In the Mail and Catalog Merge task pane, choose the merge field you want to use. Perform Step 5, 6, 7 or 8.

5 Click Address block, to insert an address block and other address options. Choose the options you want in the Insert Address Block dialog box. You can see a preview in the lower section of the dialog box. For the Match Fields button, see the first margin tip. Click OK.

6 Click Greeting line, then choose the greeting line options you want. Note: the information you choose here is only used when Publisher is unable to find the required field from the data source. Example: if a first name is required but none is provided in the data source for a record. For the Match Fields button, see the first margin tip. Click OK.

If you make a mistake when inserting a merge field/placeholder, highlight the placeholder you want to delete, then press the Delete key.

Greeting Line

Greeting line format:
Dear — Mr. Randall — ,

Greeting line for invalid recipient names:
Dear Sir or Madam,

Preview

Dear Mr. Randall,

[Match Fields...]   [OK]   [Cancel]

When creating your data source, enter the name of an image or the path to the image, but don't include the actual image itself.

7 Click Address fields, select each field you want and click Insert. For the Match Fields button, see the first margin tip. Click OK.

8 In the Mail and Catalog Merge task pane, at Step 3: Create your publication, you can also quickly insert common fields of information using the lower list box. As you move your mouse pointer over the fields, click the down arrow button on the right of the field and choose to Insert as Text or Insert as Picture.

Changing the look of merged text

You can change the look or formatting of merged text.
IMPORTANT NOTE: first format the merge fields, not the text
in the data source to which the merge fields are connected. Here's
why: when Publisher merges the text into your publication, it does
not keep the original formatting in the data source text.

Changing the format of merged text
Here's how:

1 Look in your mail merge
publication (or catalog merge
template) and highlight or
select the field that shows
the information you want to
reformat. Press the F9 key to
quickly zoom in to the
selected field.

2 Open the Format
menu and choose the
Font command.

3 Choose the options you
want in the dialog box,
as shown below, to
make your changes.

*Remember, a
merge field is a
placeholder that
represents text or
pictures that you
place into a publication.*

*In addition to
formatting, you
can also copy,
move, or delete
merge fields.*

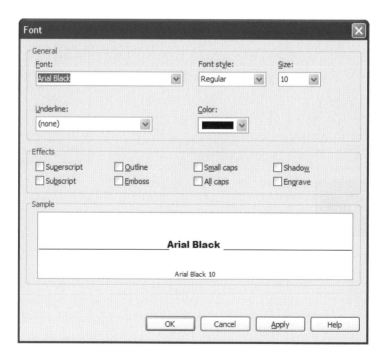

Inserting pictures as merge fields

In addition to text, images can be merged into a publication in either mail merge or catalog merge. You can insert an image as a merge field – one image for each picture merge field used. To merge from several image sources, perform the steps below:

1 Open the data source file you want. For each image that you want to include, create a new column or data field.

In Step 2, choose a meaningful name: one that makes sense to you, and which helps you identify which image the field stands for.

2 Give each new column heading a unique name. Publisher will use this name as the name of the matching merge field when you create your merge later.

3 In your data source, for each image field in each record, either enter the file name of the image you want to use, or type the path that points to where the image is located.

Remember, a path is a pointer to where a file is located. Example: C:\Documents and Settings\Jane Smith\My Documents\My Pictures\softright-logo.jpg.

4 After you have completed entering the information for each image in each record, click OK. Publisher then saves your updated data source.

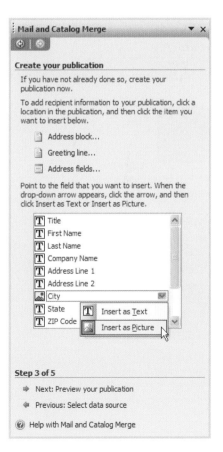

Remember, you can use an Address List to merge images as well as text. Here's how. First add the fields you need for the image information into your Address List. Then, type the path that points to the image file you want to use for each record entry in your Address List.

5 When you insert the merge fields as outlined on page 74, make sure that when you insert a merge field to represent a picture, you choose Insert as Picture, not the default, Insert as Text.

Creating a mail merge

Example data sources include: a database, spreadsheet, a Microsoft Word table, or a list of addresses (see page 66 for more information).

Open the Tools menu, choose Mail and Catalog Merge and click Mail and Catalog Merge Wizard. In the Mail and Catalog Merge task pane, under Select a merge type, make sure Mail Merge is selected. Click Next: Select a data source. Continue as follows:

1 Choose one of three options: (1) Connect to an existing compatible list of information or data source (see first margin tip); or (2) you can connect to Microsoft Outlook Contacts; or (3) create a completely new data source list in Publisher.

Publisher will automatically merge information from a data source as plain text, unless you change the setting. Therefore, to set up a merge field for a picture as a picture field, you must choose Insert as Picture when you insert the merge field.

2 In the Mail Merge Recipients dialog box, choose the recipients you want to include in your mail merge. Then, in the wizard, click Next: Create your publication.

3 In your mail merge publication, place a text box and type the text that you want to print in every instance of your final mail merge. For example, if you're creating a mail merge letter, in this step you would type the text content for the letter. Then, insert all the merge fields where you want into your publication.

Remember, during Step 4, you can also reformat your merge fields to ensure that when the information in your data source is merged, your publication looks how you want it to look. You can also, copy, move or delete a picture merge field.

4 Open the File menu and click Save As. Name your publication in the File name box and click Save. Click Next: Preview your publication.

Even if you print your mail merge, remember to save it for easy access later. You can also add the pages that have been merged, to another publication (see Publisher Help for details).

5 To preview your mail merge recipients in sequence, click the forward and back navigation buttons. You can also search for a recipient, change the list of recipients, or exclude a recipient (see facing page). Click Next: Complete the merge.

6 Now you can choose the command to print the mail merge and create the finished, merged publications (see last margin tip).

Previewing a mail merge

You can view how a mail merge publication will appear when the data is merged into it, before you run your mail merge. However, you must have first connected your merge publication to a compatible data source and inserted at least one merge field. Then, perform the steps below:

Referring to Step 2, when you preview your mail merge using the Show Merge Results command, even though you can see the actual data taken from the first record in the data source, you can't edit, reformat, move of delete the data from here.

With the merge results shown, if you want to switch back to displaying the field codes, open the Tools menu, choose Mail and Catalog Merge, and click the Show Merge Results command again. When finished, you can still check your merged data at any time, simply by clicking the Show Merge Results command in the Mail Merge menu.

To cancel a merged publication, click the Cancel Merge command in the Tools > Mail and Catalog Merge menu. Publisher prompts you one last time. Click Yes to cancel the merge.

1 With your mail merge publication displayed, open the Tools menu, choose Mail and Catalog Merge, and click the Show Merge Results command.

2 Publisher then replaces the merge fields you inserted earlier, with the information contained in the first record of your data source.

3 In the Mail and Catalog Merge task pane, under the Preview your publication section, you can now use the navigation buttons to step through and view individual records. You can also use the included links Find a recipient, Edit recipient list, or Exclude this recipient.

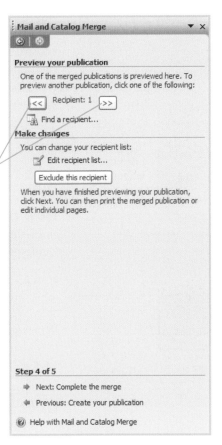

Creating a catalog merge

Catalog merge offers an ideal solution if you want to create a large catalog containing lots of items, and from which you still need to keep records of each item in a separate table, spreadsheet or database.

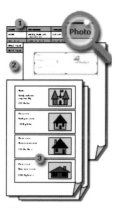

① Data source with record information, such as item names and descriptions.

② Catalog merge template with catalog merge area containing merge fields that are placeholders for record information.

③ Resulting merged pages displaying multiple records per page.

After a merge, information from the data source is inserted into each field in the catalog merge, in a repeating pattern, to ensure multiple records on each page can be displayed at the same location.

A catalog merge combines information from a data source, with a template to create pages that show multiple records on each page – such as a catalog, photo album or directory.

Introducing the catalog merge area

Just like mail merge, with catalog merge, you merge both text and pictures to create catalog merge documents. If using pictures, enter filename or path – not the image in the data source.

Publisher refers to the area in a catalog merge template into which you insert your merge fields, as the catalog merge area. After a catalog merge is done, Publisher gets the data for each field from the data source and inserts the data into each appropriate field in the merge area.

The data placed in the catalog merge area repeats as many times as necessary to display all of the new multiple records that are created as a result of the catalog merge. The step-by-step procedure below provides a clearer idea of how an entire catalog merge works.

You can insert your merge fields into your catalog merge template, during Step 3 of the Mail and Catalog Merge wizard sequence.

How to create a catalog merge

Publisher offers two main methods to create a catalog merge. You can use:

To insert merge fields, your catalog merge template must be connected to a data source, before you insert the merge fields you want.

- a predesigned catalog publication template. Here's how: display the New Publication task pane, choose Publications for Print, followed by Catalogs, then choose the catalog design you want

- the Mail and Catalog Merge wizard

The steps on the following page show how to create a catalog merge using the Mail and Catalog wizard.

If a text box within a catalog merge area is already selected when you choose to insert as text, the currently selected text box receives the new merge field automatically.

If you use one of Publisher's predefined catalog publications to create your catalog, just replace the placeholder text and images with the content you want to use. Then, if required, also change the layout, fonts and colors used in the catalog publication.

Here's two additional ways to use a completed catalog merge: (1) merge it to the end pages of an existing Publisher publication; or (2) save the catalog merge template for reuse later. This option can be especially useful if the information in the data source gets updated: you can easily create an updated catalog to match.

When adding merged pages to an existing publication, make sure that the target publication is closed before you complete the merge.

1   Open the File menu and click New. In the New Publication task pane, click Blank Print Publication (if you're creating merged pages for a web publication, click Blank Web Page). Next, open the File menu, click Page Setup, then set the page size and orientation you want to use for your final merged publication. Click OK.

2   Open the Tools menu, followed by Mail and Catalog Merge, then click Mail and Catalog Merge wizard. In the Mail and Catalog Merge task pane, under the Select a merge type, click Catalog Merge. Then click, Next: Select data source.

3   In the Mail and Catalog Merge task pane, click Browse to find the data source you want to use. Unless you choose otherwise, Publisher stores your data sources in the My Data Sources folder. Open the data source you want.

4   Publisher may display further dialog boxes, depending on the data source you choose. Make your choices. In the Catalog Records dialog box, choose the records you want to include in your catalog merge. For each record you don't want to include, clear the check boxes next to the record. Or, you can use filtering and sorting options if required – here's how: click the down arrow next to the column heading by which you want to filter. See pages 71–73 for procedures on filtering and sorting. Click OK to confirm the records that you want to include for the merge. Click Next: Create your template.

5   Now, you'll need to insert your merge fields. Click the Catalog Merge Area. Place the mouse pointer on one of the handles on the Catalog Merge Area, then drag the mouse. Insert all the merge fields into the Catalog Merge Area, where you want as shown in the wizard task pane. See pages 74–75 for more information about inserting merge fields.

When designing your catalog merge template document, limit the page length to a single page, to help ensure a reliable merge.

To reformat a merge field, first, select the merge field that you want to change – make sure you include the enclosing merge field characters («« »») – then, open the Format menu, click Font and make the changes you want.

You can move or resize the catalog merge area in your template document. Furthermore, if you move your mouse pointer over the catalog merge area, Publisher displays a ToolTip containing information showing how many times the final catalog merge repeats on the page.

6 In the Catalog Merge Area, fine adjust the positions of the text boxes or picture frames that contain the merge fields, to place each in the position you want. Also, at this stage, you can reformat the merge fields if required (see second margin tip for guidelines). Add any additional repeating text or information you want to appear close to a merge field. Click Next: Preview your catalog merge template.

7 To preview your catalog merge recipients in sequence, click the forward and back navigation buttons. You can also search for a record, edit the record list, or exclude a record.

Mail and Catalog Merge ▼ ×

Preview your catalog merge template

One of the merged records is previewed here. To preview another record, click one of the following:

[<<]   Record: 1   [>>]

Find a record...

Make changes

You can change your record list:

Edit record list...

[Exclude this record]

When you have finished previewing your catalog merge template, click Next.

8 When you're satisfied with the preview, open the File menu and choose the Save As command, type a name for your catalog merge template, and click Save. Click Next: Complete the merge.

Step 4 of 5

➡ Next: Complete the merge

⬅ Previous: Create your template

❓ Help with Mail and Catalog Merge

9 Now you have two options: (1) you can choose whether to create a new publication with the merged pages – if yes, go to Step 10. Or (2) add the merged pages to the end of an existing publication – if yes, go to Step 11.

...cont'd

After you have completed your catalog merge, if you want to add your merged pages to the end of an existing publication, both publications must share the same following traits: (1) same page size, height and width; (2) same page view (one- or two-page spread); (3) publication type: print or web; (4) page arrangement (left-to-right, or right-to-left).

When using BorderArt or applying borders to text boxes and image frames in catalog merge, use narrow border styles to ensure best results. Wide-width borders may cause overlaps or cut off key information.

If you cancel a mail merge, any merge fields other than Address Fields, Greeting Lines and Address Blocks, Publisher changes to normal text. If you cancel a catalog merge, Publisher keeps the catalog merge area and changes all other fields to normal text.

10 To create a new publication containing your merged pages, under the Merge section, click Create new publication. In the new publication window, open the File menu and click Save, type a name. Click Save to finish.

11 To add your merged pages to an existing publication, first make sure that both your catalog merge publication and existing publication match (see first margin tip). Under the Merge section, click Add to existing publication. In the Open Publication dialog box, find the publication to which you want to add your merged pages and then click Open. After Publisher opens the publication, open the File menu and click Save.

Mail and Catalog Merge

Complete the merge

Publisher is now ready to create the merged pages for your catalog. Where do you want these pages to go?

Merge

Create new publication...
Create a new publication with the merged pages.

Add to existing publication...
Add the merged pages to the end of an existing publication.

Step 5 of 5

Previous: Preview

Help with Mail and Catalog Merge

Cancelling a mail merge or a catalog merge

You can cancel a merge and disconnect either a mail merge publication or a catalog merge template, from the associated data source. Here's how. Open the Tools menu, choose Mail and Catalog Merge, then click the Cancel Merge command. Publisher asks if you want to cancel. Click Yes.

Printing a mail or catalog merge

To print a mail merge
You can print in two ways: perform either Step 1 or Step 2 below:

Before you print your mail merge, ensure your printer is set up with sufficient ink or toner, and that the printer tray has the correct sheets of labels installed.

1 To print from the Mail and Catalog Merge task pane during Step 5, complete the merge and click Print. In the Print Merge dialog box, choose the options your want. Click OK.

2 Alternatively, open the mail merge publication you want, and choose the Print Merge command on the File menu, choose the options you want and click OK.

To print a catalog merge
Perform the steps below:

You can change the size of the labels you originally specified, using the Labels option from the Page Setup command in the File menu.

1 During Step 5, complete the merge and in the Mail and Catalog Merge task pane, choose the commands you want, to tell Publisher to add your merged pages to a new publication you create, or to an existing publication.

2 Then, in the new, or existing publication, open the File menu and click Print. In the Print dialog box, choose the options you want. Click OK.

To prevent printing labels for every single address in your data source, you can apply a filter using the Filter or Sort command in the Tools > Mail and Catalog Merge menu. For example, you may want to print only those addresses from a specific state. For further information, see pages 71–73.

Print

Printer

Name: HP LaserJet 5Si/5Si MX PS   Properties...
Status: Ready
Type: HP LaserJet 5Si/5Si MX PS
Where: LPT1:
Comment: ☐ Print to file

Print range   Copies
⦿ All   Number of copies: 1 ▲▼
○ Pages from: 1 to: 1
○ Current page

Change Page Order...

Advanced Print Settings...   OK   Cancel

Creating and placing tables

Tables can help show the big picture more easily and bring some order and structure to a mass of information. This chapter explains how you can create and modify tables, including adding, deleting and changing rows and columns. We also look at how you can improve the appearance of a table by adding different types of borders, and even pictures.

Covers

Chapter Six

Creating a table

Tables can help put over varying repetitive information in a concise manner, and provide order and impact to a publication. In Publisher, you can create a variety of table styles and add images to a table.

You can also create a table using existing text in Publisher. If the text you want is already in another table, select the relevant cells. If the text is in a text box, each line of text ending with paragraph mark will form a row in your new table. Highlight all the text you want. Right-click on the highlighted text and choose Copy. Open the Edit menu and click Paste Special. In the Paste Special dialog box, under the As section, click New Table. Click OK.

You can create a table in Publisher in three main ways. Two methods are outlined in the margin tips. The third method – creating a table in Publisher – we explore below.

To create an entirely new table in Publisher, open the Objects toolbar, click the Insert Table button, then perform the steps below:

Raspberry Sorbet	
Raspberries	500g
Kirsch	1 table spoon
Water	250 ml
Sugar syrup	
Sugar	200 g
Water	250 ml

If the text you want for your table is in another table in another application, open the application and the document containing the text you want. Press Tab between each table entry in a row of text. Press Enter at the end of each row. Next, highlight the text you just prepared and press Ctrl+C. Start Publisher. Open the publication and the page you want. Open the Edit menu and click Paste Special. Under the As section, click New Table and click OK.

1 In your publication, click where you want to place your table. Publisher then displays the Create Table dialog box.

2 Choose the number of rows and columns you want, plus any optional formatting options and click OK.

3 Adjust the height and width of your table to display the size you want (see page 89 for details).

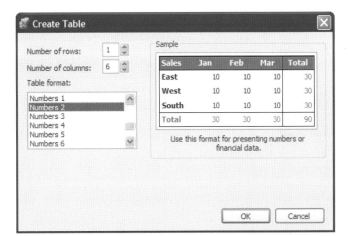

To recap, whenever you want to change or modify an item in Publisher, you must first select what you want to change, before choosing the commands to bring about the change you want.

Widget sales

4 Click in a cell in which you want to add text, and start typing. If you enter more text than a cell can hold, by default, it expands to fit the text, unless the table size is locked (see below).

You can easily tell if a table size is locked: open the Table menu and look at the Grow to Fit Text command.

If a tick mark is present, then the table is unlocked and will expand to fit your text.

If there is no tick mark, then the table size is locked. Click the command to lock or unlock the table resize status.

Selecting and moving around a table

To select a cell, row, column or an entire table, you can also use the commands in the Table > Select menu. First, click to place an insertion point in the cell, row, column or table you want to select. Then choose the command you want.

If you select a column in which any one cell is merged with another cell in an adjacent column, Publisher automatically highlights the merged column in addition to the column you select.

TABLE SELECTING OPTIONS IN PUBLISHER	
Selection target	**How**
Some text in a cell	Drag insertion point across the text
A single word	Double-click the word you want
All text in a cell	Click the cell you want, then press CTRL+A
Text in adjacent cells	Click where you wan the highlight to start, hold down SHIFT, then click where you want the highlight to end
A specific cell	Drag-select over the cells you want
Any number of neighboring cells	Drag-select over the cells you want
A single row	Move the mouse pointer near to the left side of the row you want. When the mouse pointer changes to a right-pointing arrow symbol, click the left mouse button
A single column	Move the mouse pointer near to the top of the column you want. When the mouse pointer changes to a down-pointing arrow symbol, click the left mouse button
Several rows or columns	Drag-select across the rows or columns you want
Entire table	Click in a table cell. Then open the Table menu and click Select, followed by Table

Table cell boundaries help provide a clear picture. If you can't see cell boundaries, the Boundaries and Guides command is probably switched off (no tick mark next to the command). To turn the command on, click Boundaries and Guides in the View menu.

NAVIGATING THROUGH A TABLE IN PUBLISHER	
Destination	**How**
Next cell	Press TAB or RIGHT ARROW key
Previous cell	Press SHIFT+TAB or RIGHT ARROW KEY
Up one cell / line	Press UP ARROW KEY
Down one cell / line	Press DOWN ARROW key
Any cell	Click in the desired cell
Any existing text in the table	Click the text you want
Next character	Press RIGHT ARROW key
Previous character	Press LEFT ARROW key
Next tab stop in a cell	Press CTRL+TAB

Changing row and column size

Sometimes, as you add and modify cell contents in a table, you may want to resize rows and columns to display cell contents more clearly and neatly. To resize a row or column, perform the steps below:

To resize two or more rows or columns at the same time, first highlight all the rows or columns you want to resize. Then, adjust the rows or columns as if you're adjusting a single row or column.

To change the size of a row or column

1 Place your mouse pointer over a top, bottom or side selection handle.

2 When you see the Resizer icon, drag to create the size you want.

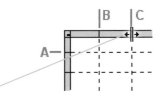

In Publisher, objects have several small shapes that mark the outline of the object. Publisher refers to these small shapes as selection handles. You drag on selection handles to resize or move an object.

To adjust the size of a table proportionately

1 Select the table you want to resize.

2 Place the mouse pointer over a corner selection handle until you see the Resizer icon: ◄╫► ╪

Widget sales

You can change how text looks in a table in the same way that you change text in Publisher generally – i.e. highlight the text you want to change, then click the button you want on the Formatting toolbar.

3 Press and hold down the Shift key.

4 Drag the selection handle to display the size of table you want. When you resize a table in this way, the proportions of all cells are affected to the same extent.

Adding and deleting rows and columns

After you've created your basic table, you may want to insert more rows or columns. Here's how. Open the Table menu, followed by Insert, then choose either Columns to the Left, Columns to the Right, Rows Above, Rows Below. Or, you can right-click the row or column you want, then from the floating menu choose the Change Table command, followed by the same commands above.

To quickly add a row at the bottom of a table, click in the lowermost right cell in the table and press the Tab key.

To insert a row or column

1 If you want to insert a single row or column, first click in the row closest to where you want to insert the new row or column.

2 If you want to insert several rows or columns at the same time, select/highlight the same number of rows or columns that you want Publisher to insert.

When you insert a row or column, Publisher places a blank row or column with the same formatting as that which you clicked or selected in Step 1.

3 Open the Table menu and choose the Insert command, followed by the row or column command you want.

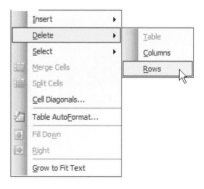

To delete a row or column

If you want to quickly select several rows or columns, hold down the Shift key, then click inside each of the rows or columns you want to highlight.

1 Select the row or column you want Publisher to delete.

2 Open the Table menu, choose the Delete command, followed by the delete option you want.

Moving and copying cell data

After developing a table, you may decide you want to move the contents of some cells, either to somewhere else within the same table, to another Publisher table, or even to another compatible Windows-based application.

To move and copy information, Publisher provides the Cut, Copy and Paste commands in the Edit menu: commands which are also accessible when clicking the right mouse button. To move cell data, carry out the steps below:

To quickly move a cell's text to another location within a table, first highlight the cell containing the text you want to move. Next, place the mouse pointer over the highlighted cell, then hold down the left mouse button and drag the highlighted text to the new cell location. Then release the mouse button.

1 If you want to move or copy cell data to another table in another Publisher document, start another session of Publisher and open the document to which you want to move the cell data. This is the target document.

2 Back in the source document, highlight the table cells containing the information you want to move or copy.

3 With the mouse pointer placed on top of the cells you want to move or copy, click the right mouse button.

To copy a table or spreadsheet from Microsoft Word or Microsoft Excel, follow these steps: (1) Open the table or spreadsheet you want to copy. (2) Select the cells you want and press Ctrl+C, to copy the cell information to the Windows Clipboard. (3) Go to your Publisher publication, open the Edit menu and click Paste.

4 On the floating menu, click the Cut command to move data or the Copy command to copy data.

5 In the destination table, if you want to replace existing cells, highlight the cells to which you want to move or copy data. But if you want to move or copy to new empty cells, click the cell in which you want the upper-left corner of the cut text to be placed.

6 Click the right mouse button.

7 On the floating menu, click Paste.

Changing how cell data looks

Publisher provides an easy way to change the format of a table, its layout and even the properties of each cell. Here's how:

1 First, select the cells you want to change.

2 Place the mouse pointer on the highlighted cells, right-click and choose the Format Table command from the floating menu.

While working on a print publication, you can even divide cells in a diagonal direction. Here's how. First, select the cells you want to change. Then, open the Table menu and click the Cell Diagonals command. Click either Divide down or Divide up, then click OK to finish.

To provide a focal point or to add visual impact to a table, you can overlay objects like icons, pictures and WordArt objects onto your table. Draw a picture frame on the table to contain your image and simply add the image to the frame. See Chapter 4 for more information.

Format Table dialog box

3 In the Format Table dialog box, choose the options you want. Across the top of the Format Table dialog box, you can choose specific options from within a tab: Colors and Lines, Size, Layout, Picture, Cell Properties, and Web. If a tab is grayed out, then no options within that tab are currently available for your table.

4 Click OK to finish and apply your new formatting changes.

Changing the color of objects

You can easily change the color of cells, rows, columns, cell text, and table borders. Also, you can change or add shading and patterns to selected cells. To change text color, follow the steps below:

1 Click the table to select it.

Population growth since 1900			
Years	Population	Years	Population
1900	96,936	1960	37,205,128
1910	367,924	1970	46,196,826
1920	1,267,490	1980	68,668,295
1930	5,829,045	1990	79,583,999
1940	17,492,594	2000	87,382,937
1950	24,719,045	2010	*

2 Highlight the desired cells.

HOT TIP

Here's another way to change the color of a table border quickly.
(1) Click the table to select it.
(2) Highlight the entire table – open the Table menu and choose Select, followed by Table.
(3) Click the table with the right mouse button and choose the Format Table command.
(4) Under the Presets section, click the middle border preset button.
(5) Under Line > Color, choose the new color you want and click OK.

3 Click the Font Color button on the Formatting toolbar, then click the desired color on the floating palette.

To change cell color, first perform Steps 1–2 above. Then carry out the steps below:

1 On the Formatting toolbar, click the Fill Color button.

2 On the floating palette, click the color you want.

3 (Optional) To see more colors, click More Fill Colors. Then click the color you want. Click OK to finish.

Merging and unmerging cells

As you develop a table, sometimes you may want to merge several cells in a specific row. For example, we often merge cells when inserting a table title or subtitle as shown in the illustrations on these pages. Cells that you choose to merge must all be in the same row or column. To merge cells, perform the procedure below:

The Merge Cells command is also available on the Table menu, when two or more adjacent cells are selected.

1 If the table is not already selected, click it.

2 Select the side-by-side cells you want to merge.

When you merge cells, you don't have to merge an entire row – just two or more highlighted cells are enough to make the Merge Cells command available (not grayed out).

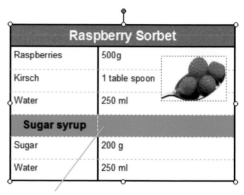

Raspberry Sorbet		
Raspberries	500g	
Kirsch	1 table spoon	
Water	250 ml	
Sugar syrup		
Sugar	200 g	
Water	250 ml	

3 Right-click on the highlighted cells.

4 From the floating menu, click the Change Table command followed by the Merge Cells command.

Cut
Copy
Paste
Delete Text
Delete Object
Save as Picture...
Change Text
Change Table   Insert
Proofing Tools   Delete
Order   Merge Cells
Format Table...   Split Cells
Wizard For This Object...   Cell Dia
Look Up...
Zoom
Hyperlink...

Raspberry Sorbet		
Raspberries	500g	
Kirsch	1 table spoon	
Water	250 ml	
Sugar syrup		
Sugar	200 g	
Water	250 ml	

If the cells you choose to merge contain text, Publisher forms each piece of text into a separate paragraph in the merged cell. If you're not happy with the result, immediately click the Undo button on the Standard toolbar and re-plan your table.

Unmerging cells

If you change your mind, you can quickly unmerge cells by first performing Steps 1–3 above. Then, on the floating menu, click the Split Cells command. Publisher then places the original content into one of the split cells.

Adding an object to a table

You can add greater visual impact to a table by adding an icon, picture, or WordArt object. However, objects you add in this way don't become part of the table in the same way as a table cell. Rather, a picture is overlaid onto a cell or several cells as shown in the illustration below. To include a picture or other object in a table, carry out the following steps:

If you want to add pictures to your table, always establish the size and layout of your table first, then add the pictures. In this way, you can ensure a picture is an appropriate match for a table, not the other way around.

1 On the Objects toolbar, click the tool you want to use to create a frame for the object you want.

2 Draw a frame on top of the table cell or cells which you want to contain your picture or other object.

3 Place the picture or object onto the frame. Pictures can be inserted using the Picture and Object commands available from the Insert menu. Apply a WordArt object using the procedures described in Chapter 3, page 54.

To make the job of moving your table and any overlaid objects easier, first select the table and all objects on it. Then, use the Group Objects command in the Arrange menu to group all selected objects together. Alternatively, click the Group Objects button.

Raspberry Sorbet	
Raspberries	500g
Kirsch	1 table spoon
Water	250 ml
Sugar syrup	
Sugar	200 g
Water	250 ml

You may need to resize and move your object to display the object in the desired position. Remember, you can use Publisher's layout guides, zoom commands and the Shift key to help accurately resize and align an object.

Applying cell and table borders

Cell boundary lines show where one cell ends and another starts. However, cell boundaries don't print. Therefore, to apply a cell border to each cell, carry out the following steps:

1 Highlight the entire table or only the cells to which you want to apply grid lines.

2 Click the right mouse button over the highlighted cells.

If you want to spice up a table, consider adding a fancy border. With the Border Style dialog box displayed, click the BorderArt tab to see the range available.

3 Click the Format Table command.

4 Under the Preset category, click Grid.

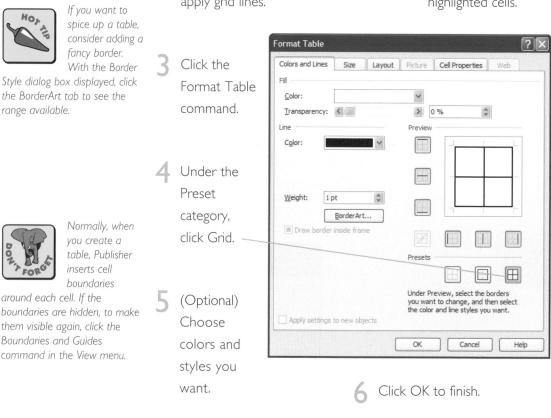

Normally, when you create a table, Publisher inserts cell boundaries around each cell. If the boundaries are hidden, to make them visible again, click the Boundaries and Guides command in the View menu.

5 (Optional) Choose colors and styles you want.

6 Click OK to finish.

Adding a table border

To add or change a border around an entire table, first highlight the cell(s) around which you want to place a border. Next, on the Formatting toolbar, click the Line/Border Style button. You can then simply click a border on the fly-out menu that appears, or click the More Styles command to display the Format Table dialog box as shown above. Click a border and optionally click another color. Finally, click OK to finish.

Crafting your designs

In this chapter, we explore how to use more of Publisher's powerful design tools to bring a designer's eye to a publication. You can discover how the delights of the Design Gallery and BorderArt Gallery can simplify your design tasks.

Covers

Chapter Seven

Brochure: an example wizard

In Chapter 1, we introduced wizards – superb "helper" guides that include many publication page design aspects for you. Here, we're going to take a closer look at a Brochure wizard.

Display the New Publication task pane when you start Publisher, or choose the New command in the File menu.

This example Brochure template has two sides. Page 1 is the brochure outside, page 2 the inside. When you print, the two pages can be printed or copied onto both sides of a single sheet of paper.

Click Publications for Print, followed by Brochures, and the brochure category you want. Continue with the steps below:

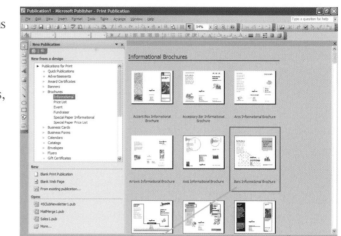

You can change your mind about the design options at any stage. Simply click the option you want under Brochure Options in the Task pane.

1 Click the wizard you want.

2 Click a text box and type your text.

Click a text frame in the wizard, to start entering the text you want to use, and double-click each graphic you want to change – Publisher prompts you to choose or search for the image you want in the Clip Art task pane.

3 Double-click a placeholder image. Choose the true image you want in the Clip Art task pane.

4 Repeat Steps 2 and 3 for all text and images you want to change.

5 Open the File menu, and click Save.

Working with Design Gallery

The Design Gallery is an excellent collection of predesigned objects that you can include in your publications. Design Gallery text and graphic objects typically include: headline and masthead designs, pull-quotes, forms, table of contents designs, logos, advertisements and calendars.

Many of the objects are designed to match the styles used in Publisher wizards. For example, if you used the Brochure wizard, the Design Gallery can offer alternatives by matching components to include with, or instead of, objects already placed.

You can also store design elements which you create in the Design Gallery, providing easy access later. Publisher also makes the job of finding your design elements simple by grouping related objects into categories. If you can't find the right category in which to store an object, simply create a new category to suit your needs.

To open the Design Gallery, simply click the Design Gallery Object button on the Objects toolbar. Publisher then displays the opening Design Gallery dialog box, as shown below:

The Design Gallery provides an excellent platform on which you can combine your own ideas and try different combinations to see which produces the kind of results you want.

By default, Publisher ensures the Design Gallery contains objects that are relevant to the type of publication you're working on. For example, if you're creating a Web page, you'll find Web page objects available, but if you're working on a print-based publication, web page objects won't be available.

Objects that you add to the Design Gallery using the My Objects tab, are not, by default, available to any other Publisher documents. However, you can import a Design Gallery into any publication at any time.

The Design Gallery Object button on the Objects Toolbar

A selected Design Gallery object

Here's how to import an object into the Design Gallery.
(1) Click to select the object you want to import.
(2) Click the Design Gallery Object button on the Objects toolbar.
(3) Click the My Objects tab.
(4) Click Options, followed by Add Selection to Design Gallery.
(5) In the Add Object dialog box, type a name for your object in the Object name box.
(6) Choose or create a category.
(7) Click OK.

In the Design Gallery, if you delete an object by mistake, simply close the current publication without saving it, then reopen the publication – the "deleted" object will still be available.

Publisher records the changes you've made to the Design Gallery when you save the current publication. Therefore, save immediately after making any important Design Gallery changes.

Choosing a Design Gallery object

To add an object from the Design Gallery to your publication, first click the Design Gallery Object button on the Objects toolbar. Click the tab you want: by category, by design or view your own design elements in My Objects. Next, click the category you want in the left column. In the right column, double-click the design object you want, or click the Insert Object button.

Creating and renaming Design Gallery categories

Display the My Objects tab as described above. Click the Options button, followed by Edit Categories. In the Edit Categories dialog box click the buttons you want to rename, or create a new category.

Deleting a Design Gallery object

You can delete objects that you store in the Design Gallery listed under the My Objects tab, for the publication you're currently working on. However, you can't delete any of Publisher's own Design Gallery objects – that is those available from the Objects by Category and Objects by Design tabs. To delete an object, right-click the object you want to delete, then from the floating menu, choose the Delete this object command. Or click the Options button and choose the same command.

Creating a logo

In Publisher, you can create a logo entirely from scratch or you can use the logo wizard to make the job a little easier, or simply to gain some inspirational ideas. To create a logo using a Publisher wizard, carry out the steps below:

After Step 3, when you select your logo, Publisher places the wizard button near to your logo. You can click the wizard button and change the options you want in the task pane.

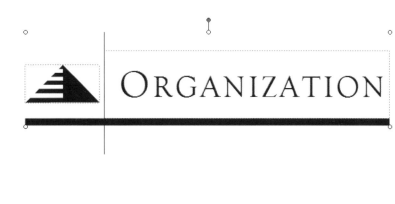

When working with a logo, you can maintain the brand while making the appearance of a logo more subtle. Here's how. Make a copy of your logo and convert it into a watermark-type graphic. Then place the watermark in the background on a master page. See page 106 for more details.

1 On the Objects toolbar (as shown on page 99), click the Design Gallery Object button.

2 In the Objects by Category tab, under the Categories section, click Logos.

3 Under the Logos section, double-click the logo style you want to use. Publisher inserts your chosen logo style onto the page.

Any logos that you create using the Design Gallery cannot be used with personal information sets (see Chapter 3, page 53).

4 If necessary, zoom in or press F9, so that you can see the placeholder text in the logo more clearly. Click the placeholder text, then type the text you want to insert.

5 If you want to replace the placeholder picture in the logo, first click the picture frame. Next, right-click on the picture, choose the Change Picture command from the floating menu, then click the command you want (see also, first margin tip).

Using the BorderArt Gallery

You can add BorderArt to any rectangular shapes you create in Publisher, including picture, text, table and WordArt frames.

The BorderArt Gallery includes over 150 plain and fancy borders, which you can use to transform an otherwise dull object into something more memorable. To apply BorderArt, first, click to select the object you want. Next, open the Format menu and click the AutoShape command, then carry out the steps below:

1 In the Format AutoShape dialog box, click the BorderArt button.

2 Click a new border or click Create Custom to create a custom border.

To create ornate or unusual bullets, first, draw a box with the Rectangle tool on the Objects toolbar. Next, on the Formatting toolbar, click the Line/Border Style button followed by the More Lines command. In the Format AutoShape dialog box, under the Line section, click the BorderArt button and choose your desired border. Click OK twice. On your publication page, reduce the size of the box, until it occupies a single frame of the design or is the bullet size you want.

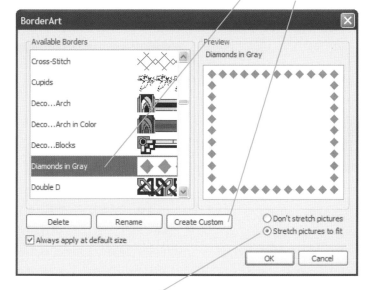

3 (Optional) Choose whether or not pictures may be stretched.

Some shapes can't have BorderArt applied to them, like shapes drawn with the Oval tool or AutoShapes tool. If the selected shape is not compatible with BorderArt, Publisher doesn't provide access to the BorderArt tab.

4 (Optional) Choose the color and line/border weight you want.

5 Click OK to finish.

Deleting a border

If you want to remove a border entirely, click the object whose border you want to remove. Click the Line/Border Style button on the Formatting toolbar, followed by the No Line command. Publisher then replaces the border with a light outline of the object.

Wrapping text around an object

If you're short of text space, wrapping text around the outline of a picture, can create more space for your text, and provide a more interesting design feature.

Publisher provides several options to allow you to control how text wraps around an object. However, the kind of text wrap described on this page and the following page only works for print publications. You can:

- wrap text around an object's frame
- wrap text around the outline of a graphic object located inside a frame
- customize the way text wraps around an object
- prevent text from wrapping around an object

Wrapping text around an image frame
Perform the following steps:

The boundary shown around a text-wrapped object does not print – it simply identifies the wrap outline.

1 Click to select the picture frame you want.

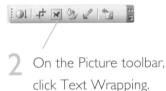

2 On the Picture toolbar, click Text Wrapping.

3 Click Square.

Inside Story Headline

The following text consists of a mock Latin which has been based upon the average frequency of characters and word lengths of the English language in order to reproduce a reasonably accurate overall visual impression. Lorem ipsum dolor sit amet, consectetur adipscing elit, sed diam nonnumy eiusmod tempor incidunt ut labore et dolore magna aliquam erat volu- est er expedit distinct. Nam liber a tempor cum soluta nobis eligend optio com- que nihil quod a impedit anim id quod maxim placeat facer possim omnis es volup- tas assumenda est, omnis do- lor repellend. Temporem autem quinsud et aur office debit aut tum rerum necesit atib saepe

Wrapping text around the outline of an object
By wrapping text around the outline of a picture or WordArt object rather than its rectangular frame, you can create a more stylish look. This approach can work especially well when the graphic object contains some element of action, tension or emotion as shown in the illustration above.

If you've chosen text wrap, but Publisher refuses to wrap text around a graphic object, the selected graphic may be set up as transparent. Try pressing Ctrl+T to make the graphic opaque. Also, Publisher cannot wrap text around a picture or a WordArt object in a table.

To wrap text around the outline of a graphic object or picture, perform Steps 1 and 2 above, then click the wrap button option you want other than Square. Overleaf, we explore how to customize text wrap around an object even more accurately to achieve that special finish.

Square
Tight
Through
Top and Bottom
None
Edit Wrap Points

Changing the text wrap shape

You can customize the text wrap and trace the outline of the image more closely than the methods explored on the previous page. You can also change the amount of space between a picture or other object and the text which wraps around it. Here's how:

To prevent text from wrapping around objects, first click the text frame you want. Next, open the Format menu and choose the Text Box command. In the Format Text Box dialog box, click the Layout tab and under Wrapping Style, click None. Click OK to finish.

1 Select the picture frame containing the picture you want to change.

2 Open the Arrange menu, then place your mouse pointer on Text Wrapping – ensure Square is not selected.

3 From the Arrange menu, place your mouse pointer on Text Wrapping, then click Edit Wrap Points.

When reshaping the text wrap around a picture or WordArt object, if you want to delete an adjust handle, hold down the Ctrl+Shift keys while you click the handle you want to delete.

4 Publisher places adjust handles around the picture border. You may need to zoom in to see the adjust handles properly.

que·nihil·quod·a·im
anim·id·qu
maxim·pl
facer·pos
omnis·es
tas·assu
est,·om
lor·repe

Picture

5 Place your mouse pointer over the border of the picture until you see the Adjust pointer, then drag the pointer. As you drag, Publisher changes the shape of the image border.

If Publisher refuses to wrap text around the outline of a graphic, check if the frame is surrounded by BorderArt. If you want text to wrap around the outline of a graphic, remove any BorderArt present.

6 If you want to insert additional Adjust handles, place your mouse pointer somewhere on the border where you want to insert a new handle, press and hold down the Ctrl key, then click. Drag the new Adjust handle to where you want. To delete an Adjust handle, press and hold down Ctrl+Shift while you click the Adjust handle you want to delete.

Working with pages

Elsewhere in this book, we've explored working with text, pictures and various design aids. This chapter looks at creating and manipulating your publications at page level, and how you can build in consistency throughout longer publications.

Covers

Creating master pages

In Publisher, you place on master pages those items that you want to repeat on multiple pages; for example: headers and footers. Every new publication has at least one master page called a single-page master. You can also have a two-page master, and convert a two-page master to a single-page master, or convert a single-page master into a two-page master. You can create a completely new master page or copy an existing one and even further modify the copied master page to precisely get the finish you want.

To move to a master page from a publication page, open the View menu and click the Master Page command – Publisher places a tick mark next to the command. To move back to a publication page, click the Master Page command again.

Moving an object from a master page to a publication page

First, open the View menu and click Master Page. Next, in the Master Page task pane, click the down-arrow next to the master page that contains the object you want to move to a publication page. Click Edit. Then, on the master page, select the object you want to move. Open the Arrange menu and click Send to Foreground. Click OK in the alert message box.

To move an object from a publication page to a master page

Display the publication page that contains the object you want to move. Select the object you want. Open the Arrange menu and click Send to Master Page. Click OK in the alert message box.

How to change a single-page master page to a two-page master page

First, open the View menu and click Master Page. Next, look in the Edit Master Pages task pane, then click the down-arrow next to the single-page master page that you want to convert to a two-page master page. In the drop-down menu, click the Change to Two-page command.

Publisher copies all objects that are on the single-page master page to the new page just created. Furthermore, Publisher takes the left and right margin settings from the single-page master, and installs them as the inner and outer margins in the new two-page master.

Viewing a two-page spread

Many multi-page publications, like the newsletter shown below for instance, require printing on both sides of the paper. When you're viewing a publication on the screen with two pages side by side – just like this book – Publisher considers this form of layout as a two-page spread.

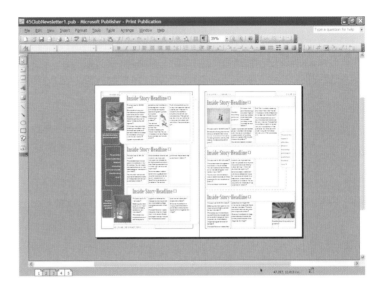

If a publication has three or more pages, you can opt to view facing pages side by side, as a two-page spread. To do this, open View menu and click Two-Page Spread. To switch back to single page view, open the View menu and click the command again to clear the tick mark.

Two-page spread design considerations

When establishing the structure of a document containing facing pages, it's a good idea to apply some special consideration to the design. For example, consider the following:

- documents with facing pages generally need wider inner margins to allow for the folding or binding after the document is printed

- decide whether you want the left and right pages to look the same in terms of layout, or whether you want each to mirror the other

Changing page size and margins

Your publication page size can be different to the paper page size. Paper page size is the size of paper you choose to print on, for example, Letter or A4. Publication page size is the size you specify for your publication. Example: your publication size may be A3, made up of printed A4 sheets, which you could then take to a printer to create the final product.

To change the publication size

Open the File menu and click Page Setup. Click the Layout tab, and under Publication type, click the type of publication you want. Choose or type or page size. For any Custom option, you can enter the page size you want. Click OK.

To change the paper size

Open the File menu and click Page Setup. For this option, click the Printer and Paper tab. Under the Paper section, in the Size box, click the size of paper you want to use. Click OK.

To change the page orientation of the publication

Open the File menu and click Page Setup followed by the Layout tab. Under the Orientation section, if you want a page that is taller than it is wide (vertical), click Portrait. If you want a page that is wider than it is tall (horizontal), click Landscape. Click OK.

About page margins

The spaces at the top, bottom, left and right edges of your pages are your page margins. These spaces are outside of the area where you place text or graphics. Publisher identifies the inner edge of page margins with non-printing dotted lines.

To change your page margins

Open the Arrange menu and click Layout Guides. With the Margin Guides tab displayed, under the Margin Guides section, set your new left, right, top and bottom margins. Click OK.

Displaying and hiding margin guides

If you can't see a margin guide, it may be hidden behind opaque objects. If you can't see any guides, Boundaries and Guides in the View menu may be switched off (no tick mark). To re-display page margins and other guides and boundaries, open the View menu and click Boundaries and Guides (tick mark = active command).

Using layout and ruler guides

Publisher provides non-printing layout guides and ruler guides to help you align text and graphic objects accurately. Use layout guides on master pages to create a grid framework of rows and columns on which to plan your publication.

Each layout guide you insert repeats on every page. Publisher provides four types of layout guide: Margin, Column, Row and Baseline. You can use Baseline guides to help precisely align text across adjacent columns. Margin, Column and Row guides appear as blue dotted lines; Baseline guides as gold dotted lines. You can drag ruler guides onto individual pages when required. Ruler guides appear as green dotted lines.

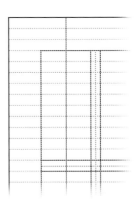

To insert a layout guide

Open the Arrange menu and click Layout Guides. Click the Grid Guides tab and set the number of columns and rows you need to create the design grid you want. Click OK.

To change baseline guides

Open the Arrange menu and click Layout Guides, followed by the Baseline Guides tab. Choose the new values you want. Click OK.

To apply a ruler guide

Place your mouse pointer onto a vertical or horizontal ruler. When the mouse pointer changes to the Adjust pointer (see third margin tip), drag a ruler guide onto the page to where you want. To move or delete a ruler guide, first place the mouse pointer over the ruler guide you want to move or delete. When you see the Adjust pointer, drag the guide to where you want – or completely off the page to delete the guide.

Snapping to guides and rulers

On the Arrange menu, the Snap > to Ruler Marks, Snap > to Guides, and Snap > to Objects commands, can also help align and keep objects in place (see second margin tip). To turn a Snap To command off, simply click the desired command to hide the tick mark that was placed next to it.

Creating headers and footers

Headers and footers contain text and graphic information about your publication, like page numbers, publication or section title, horizontal lines, and so on. Headers are placed at the top of a page and footers at the bottom.

Here's a quick way to have Publisher ignore headers, footers and other background items on specific pages. This feature is particularly useful if you don't want headers and footers to appear on the first page of your publication. Display the page you want, then open the View menu and click Ignore Master Page.

When adding page numbers, if you type a number instead of inserting the page number marker, Publisher places that same number on every page when you return to normal view.

Add a header or footer to a master page (single)

Open the View menu and click Header and Footer. From the Header and Footer toolbar, click the button options you want, type any associated text you want and format your header and footer text. When finished, on the Header and Footer toolbar, click Close.

Adding headers and footers to facing pages

Open the View menu and click Master Page. In the Edit Master Pages task pane, click the down-arrow button next to the single master page you want, and click Edit. Perform the same steps in

the previous section to create a header or footer. In the Edit Master Pages task pane, click the down-arrow button next to the master page you're currently changing, then click Change to Two-page. Edit your headers and footers as required. When finished, on the Edit Master Pages toolbar, click Close Master View.

Hiding a header and footer

First create a copy of a master page as outlined on page 106. Next, delete the header or footer on the master page copy. Finally, apply this new copied master page to the publication page on which you want the header or footer hidden.

Adding and removing page numbers

Open the View menu and click Master Page. In the Edit Master Pages task pane, move your mouse pointer to the master page on which you want to add or remove page numbers, click the down-arrow button, then Edit.

Open the Insert menu and click Page Numbers. In the Page Numbers dialog box, make your choices and click OK. Publisher inserts a hash symbol (#) as the page number marker on the master page. Click View > Master Page again, to return to normal view. The page number markers now appear as true page numbers. To delete page numbers from a master page, first select the header or footer containing the page number marker (#), then press the Delete key.

Adding, moving and deleting a page

When adding or deleting pages, first make sure that you are in normal view (not viewing a master page). In normal view, when you open the View menu, no tick mark is placed next to the Master Page command.

If the page you want to delete, contains any text or graphic objects that you want to keep, drag those items onto Publisher's non-printing workspace area before you delete the page(s).

To add a page

Move to the page nearest to where you want to add extra pages. Next, open the Insert menu and click the Page command. In the Insert Page dialog box, choose the options you want and click OK. When you insert a page, Publisher copies any text, graphics or guides placed on the master page, to your new page.

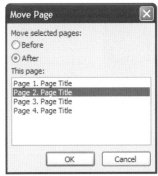

For any page you delete, only the text and objects that are unique to that page are deleted. Before actual deletion, Publisher moves any text that connects to text boxes on other pages, to another page.

To create a copy of an entire page

Move your mouse pointer to the page sorter situated in the lower left corner of the main Publisher window. Right-click on the page(s) you want to copy, then click Insert Duplicate Page. Publisher inserts the copied page(s) immediately after the page on which you right-clicked.

Moving a page

Move your mouse pointer to the page sorter situated in the lower left corner of the main Publisher window. Right-click on the page(s) you want to move and choose the Move Page command. In the Move Page dialog box, choose the options you want, then click OK.

If you want to delete the contents of a page and not the actual page itself, simply select all the objects on the page and then press the Delete key.

Deleting a page

Display the page you want to delete. Open the Edit menu, and click the Delete Page command. If you're viewing a two-page spread, Publisher displays the Delete Page dialog box. Choose the options you want and click OK.

Exploring color schemes

To change, create or customize a color scheme, you can open the Format menu and click Color Schemes.

A color scheme is a special group of colors that are associated with a publication. When you start a new publication, a default "standard" color scheme is applied to your publication. You can also define your own custom color schemes. To see the current scheme colors, click the down-arrow button next to Fill Color button on the Formatting toolbar.

Here are some useful definitions to learn. A tint is any color that contains a percentage of white. A shade contains one measure of the original color and nine measures of black. A pattern is any simple design characteristic that repeats, such as a grid or net. A gradient is made up tints or shades that create a finish in which one side has increased shading.

Choosing a color from the current color scheme

To fill an object with a color from the scheme color set, first select the object. On the Formatting toolbar, click the Fill Color button. Under the Scheme Colors category, click the color you want.

Changing to another color scheme

In the Color Schemes task pane, Publisher displays the current color scheme selected. To choose another color scheme, click the color scheme you want. Publisher then changes all the objects in your publication to show the colors in the new color scheme.

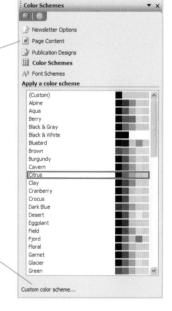

Colors that make up standard color schemes that come with Publisher, are carefully chosen so that relative colors match together. Standard color schemes are always available in the Color Schemes task pane.

Creating a custom color scheme

Towards the lower part of the Color Schemes task pane, click the Custom color scheme link. In the Color Schemes dialog box, for each color you want to change, click the down-arrow button next to each color and choose a new color. To see more colors, click the More Colors button, then click the color you want from either the Standard or Custom tab, and click OK. If you want a shade, click Fill Effects and choose the shade you want. Click Save Scheme, type a unique name for your color scheme, and click OK.

If you've already filled an object with a color from the publication color scheme, and decide to change the original color in the color scheme, Publisher changes the fill colors of any objects filled with the original color to that of the new color.

Publisher then applies the new colors in your new custom color scheme to all the objects that were filled with the colors from the original color scheme. Also, Publisher includes your custom color scheme in the list of standard color schemes.

Checking your document for errors

You're almost ready to print or publish but before you do, in this chapter, we examine how to use Publisher's powerful document-checking tools to help ensure that your text, and the design and layout of your publication are perfect every time.

Covers

Chapter Nine

How to check text spacing

After you've entered text into a publication, you can use Publisher to check for more than one character space between words. Most proportionally-spaced fonts today are designed so that you no longer need to insert two spaces at the end of a sentence: one is adequate. Furthermore, with justified text, two spaces after a full stop can cause unsightly "rivers of white space" appearing throughout your document when printed.

To search your text for double (or more) spaces after words, first open the Edit menu and click the Replace command. Then, carry out the steps below:

You can find and replace any text, and also fine tune your searches further in the Find options using the Match whole word only and Match case check boxes.

When performing general find and replace, Publisher can find text in overflow sections, but not in Continued notices within connected text boxes, or text within data fields (such as those in Mail and Catalog Merge, or web page forms).

You can also use Publisher's powerful Search and Replace tool to quickly replace multiple occurrences of a word or phrase.

1 In the Find and Replace dialog box, click here and press the Spacebar twice to enter two spaces.

2 Press the Tab key to move the insertion point to the Replace with box.

3 In the Replace with box, press the Spacebar once.

4 Ensure "All" is displayed here. If not, click the drop-down arrow button to correct the setting.

5 Click the Replace All button to replace all detectable instances of double spaces within your publication.

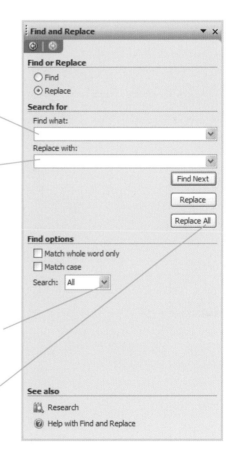

Correcting errors while you type

Even the best typists make errors occasionally. We may type "nad" when we really meant to type the word "and". However, Publisher provides AutoCorrect: a great tool that can help correct misspelled words, capitalization mistakes and even grammatical errors.

Using AutoCorrect

By default, AutoCorrect is turned on, so as you type, AutoCorrect monitors your work in the background, and replaces each instance of an incorrect word, with what it considers to be the correct version. If AutoCorrect is unsure about a word, it places a wavy red line underneath each suspect word. To fix a suspect word, first right-click it, then choose the option you want from the menu list.

Before using AutoCorrect, make a list of words or phrases that you often misspell; make sure that you write each word or phrase exactly in its misspelled form. Next, open the Tools menu, choose AutoCorrect Options and then carry out the steps below:

To correct errors while you type, in the Check Spelling dialog box, the "Check spelling as you type" check box must contain a tick mark. Here's how to display the Check Spelling dialog box: on the main menu bar, choose Tools > Spelling > Spelling Options.

Whenever you're typing text in Publisher, try to get into the habit of being aware when you enter text incorrectly. Once a pattern is identified, that's the ideal time to enter it into Publisher's AutoCorrect feature while the event is fresh in your mind.

In additions to correcting text, you can also use AutoCorrect to insert special graphics or symbols. For example, if you type "(c)", AutoCorrect inserts a true copyright symbol ©, or automatically enter typographer's quotes instead of straight quotes..

1 Choose the options you want.

2 Click here to set additional options like hyphens and curly (smart) quotes.

3 Click here to enter exceptions, like acronyms.

4 Enter each misspelled word here.

5 Enter the correct version of each word here.

6 Click OK to record your changes.

Checking spelling

To check spelling, first click in the first text or table frame, or AutoShape that you want to check. Next, open the Tools menu and choose Spelling, followed by the Spelling command. Publisher then displays the Check Spelling dialog box only if it finds an unrecognized word. If the Check Spelling dialog box does not appear, no misspellings could be found and the spell check is complete:

> For each word that Publisher displays in the Not in dictionary box, choose the option you want, either from the list of alternatives displayed, or from the buttons on the right.

Options include: ignore this word, ignore all instances of this word, change the word, change all instances, or Add to the dictionary (so the word won't be flagged again).

If you want to change the way Publisher automatically hyphenates words, first click in the text block you want to hyphenate. Then, open the Tools menu and click the Language command followed by the Hyphenation command. Next, choose your desired options and click the OK button. Any connected text blocks in a chain are also re-hyphenated.

Check Spelling: English (U.S.)

Not in dictionary:

    nad

Change to: and
Suggestions: and
                nod
                mad
                nard
                nerd
                nab

[Ignore] [Ignore All]
[Change] [Change All]
[Add]   [Close]

☑ Check all stories

2 To check every text box, table frame and AutoShape in your publication, click here (place a tick).

3 (Optional) Choose Close to stop the spell check before it has finished.

Changing spelling options

You can change how you want Publisher to manage a spell check. Open the Tools menu, choose Spelling, followed by Spelling Options. Then click to clear or select the check boxes you want to change. Click the OK button to finish.

Spelling Options

☑ Check spelling as you type
☑ Flag repeated words
☐ Suggest from main dictionary only
☑ Ignore words in UPPERCASE
☑ Ignore words with numbers
☑ Ignore Internet and file addresses

[OK] [Cancel]

Using Design Checker

Publisher provides Design Checker to help you check the layout of a publication and identify any design and printing problems. Design Checker may offer to fix an error automatically, or you may have to fix the error manually. You can check specific pages or an entire publication. To start the Design Checker, open the Tools menu and click Design Checker, then carry out the steps below:

During Step 2, Publisher usually also provides an option to go to the page where the problem lies. You can then fix the problem directly using the guidelines in Design Checker.

After a document has been checked once using Design Checker, Publisher may display a dialog box asking if you want to run the Design Checker again, to make sure no further layout errors exist. Click Yes to start the Design Checker or No to end the session.

1 In the Design Checker task pane, click the arrow next to the item you want to fix.

2 From the drop-down menu, click the option to automatically fix the problem (also, see first margin tip).

3 Choose the command Never Run this Check Again if you want stop the check for all instances of this problem.

4 Choose the Explain command to see suggestions about how to fix the current problem.

5 (Optional) Click here to display the Design Checker Options dialog box, and make your changes using the General and Checks tabs.

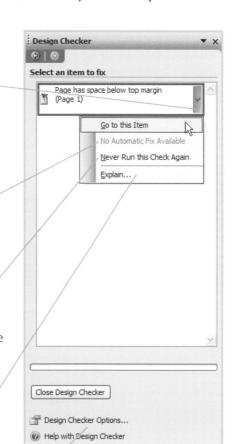

Previewing before printing

When you reach this stage, you've come a long way. Congratulations! Now you can view your masterpiece on the screen as it will look when printed. Perform the following steps to preview your publication before printing:

1 Open File menu.

2 Choose the Print Preview command.

3 Use the buttons on the toolbar to examine and move around your publication.

4 You can easily see what each button does: simply place the mouse pointer on a button and a hint/tooltip caption appears.

5 (Optional) If you're ready to print, you can choose the Print button to print your document.

6 When finished, click the Close button to exit Print Preview.

Printing to a desktop printer

In terms of power, quality, flexibility and low cost, today's desktop printers are simply amazing! In this chapter, we examine what's involved in printing to a desktop printer, and explore some ways in which to tackle common printing problems.

Covers

Chapter Ten

Setting up and using a desktop printer

Final check list before you print

1. Confirm that when you first started your publication, you established the target printer to which you want to print your publication.

To quickly print an entire publication without displaying the Print dialog box and without changing any default print options, click the Print button on the Standard toolbar, as shown below:

2. Run the spell checker as outlined on page 116.

3. Run Design Checker as outlined on page 117.

4. Preview your publication as described on page 118.

5. Examine each page with Boundaries and Guides turned off, so that you can see your publication without any distractions (see page 108 for more details).

6. Make sure your printer is stocked with sufficient paper and ink and that the printer is ready to print.

To print to a desktop printer

Open the File menu and click Print. In the Print dialog box, choose the options you want, then click OK.

You can change or specify further choices for your printer, including paper size, graphics and color options (if applicable) by clicking the Properties button and making your choices in the dialog boxes.

To print on non-standard-sized paper, first open the File menu, click Page Setup, followed by the Printer and Paper tab. Then, under the Paper section, click the paper size you want. Next, in the Source box, click Manual feed (if available), followed by OK.

To print specific pages only

Open the File menu and click Print. Under the Print range section, choose the page range you want to print in the Pages from and to boxes. To print a single page, enter the same page number in both the "Pages from" and "to" boxes. Click OK.

To print a draft copy of a publication

Open the File menu and click Print. Click Advanced Print Settings. In the Advanced Print Settings dialog box, click the Graphics and Fonts tab. Under the Graphics section, click Do not print any graphics. Click OK. Click OK again.

Printing to both sides of the paper at the same time

If your printer supports double-sided (duplex) printing, open the File menu and click Print. In the Print dialog box, click the Properties button. Click the Layout tab. Under the Print on Both Sides section, choose the option you want. Click OK, twice.

To cancel printing in Microsoft Windows

While a document is printing, Windows displays a Printer icon in the Windows task bar. However, for short publications, the Printer icon may only appear in the Task bar for a few seconds. Double-click the Printer icon. Click the publication you want to cancel. Open the Document menu and click Cancel. If Windows asks if you really want to cancel, Click Yes.

If you're using an outside print shop to print your final publication, or you simply want to move your entire publication to another computer, you can use the Pack and Go command on the File menu to ensure all the essential components, including fonts, etc. are copied correctly.

Printing the date and time

You can set Publisher to insert the current date and time – especially useful to help keep track of multiple publication drafts.

By using the Print Date or Time option, you can keep a permanent log of all your printouts. This can be useful when verifying dates and times with printers and work colleagues.

Here's how. First, click in the text box (or table) where you want the date and time to appear, or

Date and Time

Available formats:	Language:
5/21/2004	English (U.S.)
Friday, May 21, 2004	
May 21, 2004	
5/21/04	
2004-05-21	
21-May-04	
5.21.2004	
May. 21, 04	
21 May 2004	
May 04	
May-04	
5/21/2004 5:50 PM	
5/21/2004 5:50:53 PM	

☐ Update automatically

Default...   OK   Cancel

draw a new text frame where you want. Next, open the Insert menu and click Date and Time. In the Date and Time dialog box, choose the Format and Language options you want. Make sure Update automatically is selected. Then click OK. When you print, Publisher prints the current date and time at the location you set.

Working with special paper

If you've not chosen to use an outside printer, you can still create a stylish, professional, colored finish to your publications, without having to pay the higher costs that are often associated with using several colors. How? You could try using preprinted colored paper stock from PaperDirect or Avery.

Publisher includes a range of electronic templates that represent a variety of these papers, patterns and styles from PaperDirect and Avery, so that you can view how a specific publication template design will appear when printed. To use special paper, first open the View menu and click Special Paper. Then follow the steps below:

Printing using the special paper option is an excellent way to create a consistent and stylish corporate identity including business cards, complement slips, letterheads, and so on, at a modest price.

In the Special Paper dialog box, Publisher lists the styles available for several types of publication. When you select a style, Publisher places a small preview image in the lower part of the dialog box.

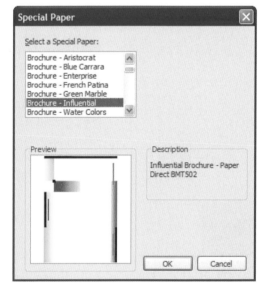

1 In the Special Paper dialog box, under Select a special paper, click the paper style you want.

2 Click OK when finished. Publisher then applies the style of paper you chose to the current publication.

3 Now, add the text and graphics you want for the rest of the publication, then click Save.

To stop using special paper and clear the screen, first open the View menu and click Special Paper. Next, under the Select a Special Paper category, click None, then click OK. Publisher removes the special paper style from the publication.

4 When you're ready to print, first make sure you have a sufficient quantity of the paper style that you chose in Step 2 installed in your printer.

5 Open the File menu and click Print.

Printing labels and envelopes

To print envelopes manually

1 Open the File menu and click Page Setup.

2 In the Page Setup dialog box, click the Printer and Paper tab.

3 Under the Paper category, in the Size list, click the size of envelope you want.

4 In the Source list, click the paper source you want. The specific choices available here vary from printer to printer. If possible, click Manual Feed or Envelope Feeder, then click OK.

At Step 5 opposite, make sure you have a supply of the correct envelopes easily accessible, before you choose to print.

5 Open the File menu and click Print.

6 In the Print dialog box, choose the options you want and click OK.

7 Insert the first envelope into your printer feeder as stated in your specific printer guide. Print your envelopes.

Printing labels using Page Setup

Although you can print labels using one of Publisher's wizard templates, if you want to see a wider range of label sizes, consider using the method below:

During Step 4 opposite, when you select your label type, Publisher provides a snapshot of the label page in the preview window.

1 Open the File menu and click New.

2 Open the File menu and click Page Setup, to set up your new publication.

3 Under Publication Type, select Label.

4 Under Page Size, choose the label type you want for your publication. Publisher provides 90 different types of Avery labels.

5 Click OK.

Troubleshooting print problems

Using the Print Troubleshooter

If your publication doesn't print the way you expect, or won't print at all, you can use Publisher's Print Troubleshooter. Here's how. Open the Tools menu and click Options, followed by the Print tab. Then click Automatically display Print Troubleshooter to place a tick mark in the check box, then click OK. When you next print, Publisher can help you identify where the problem lies.

If you can't print anything, always run a printer self-test first. This checks that the printer is capable of printing as a standalone device (i.e. not getting information from your PC).

Using Publisher Help

You can also get additional help on fixing printing problems, using Publisher Help. Here's how. First, click the task pane down-arrow button, then click Help.

If you can't see the task pane, open the View menu and click Task Pane.

Make sure that you have the correct printer driver installed. A printer driver is a small software program that allows Publisher to communicate with your printer. Check your Windows documentation or Help for more details.

In the Search for box, type: print troubleshooter. Then click the search button. Publisher then displays lots of links with remedies to various printing problems. You can also access Publisher Help online (see the Help menu).

Search Results ▼ ✕

20 results

- Troubleshoot printing scanned pictures
- Troubleshoot printing a poster, banner, or other large publication
- Troubleshoot using crop and bleed marks
- Troubleshoot printing publications on a desktop printer
- Troubleshoot corrupted graphics
- Troubleshoot desktop printer settings
- Troubleshoot printing labels on a desktop printer
- Troubleshoot printing business cards
- Troubleshoot printing a two-page layout or booklet
- Troubleshoot fonts and subsetting
- Troubleshoot editing pictures
- Troubleshoot layout guides, ruler guides, and the ruler
- Troubleshoot working with frames and pictures
- Troubleshoot using PaperDirect or Avery patterned papers
- Troubleshoot linked graphics
- About accessibility for people with disabilities

Search

Offline Help

print troubleshooter

Can't find it?

Checking printer spool settings

Ideally, try to ensure you have at least 150–200 Mb of spare hard drive space. If you have less and your publication file size is large, then you may have print problems. Try freeing up some hard disk space by deleting unwanted information (or copying files to another location) to free up space.

If you have trouble printing, consider changing your printer's spool settings. Normally, when you print, your file information is stored in a special holding area on your PC's hard disk. Sending information this way to a printer is called spooling. Normally, spooling is turned on. Try turning the setting off and printing again. See your Windows documentation for details.

Commercial color printing

Publisher 2003 supports both spot color and process color printing, and includes the key tools a commercial printing service needs to turn your Publisher document into a smart, commercially printed product. In this chapter, we explore what you need to do to make it all happen!

Covers

Chapter Eleven

Commercial printing checklist

Preparing your publication

Create your own simple document production plan – a plain text file is sufficient. Prepare and proofread your publication properly before you present it to your printer. Check spelling and grammar. Use Design Checker. Use Graphics manager. If you're delivering your publication to your printer in Publisher format, use Pack and Go on the File menu.

Ten key guidelines to discuss with your printer

A Service Bureau prepares your publication for printing on a commercial printing press.

If your commercial printer requires you to send your publication to them in Adobe Portable Document Format (PDF), remember, you'll need to have Adobe Acrobat Distiller software installed on your PC, to convert your publication to the correct format.

Consider carefully, whether to use patterns in your color schemes within a publication designed for commercial printing. Why? Patterns take longer to process from file to film and so can push up your printing costs.

1. Before you start work on your publication, discuss the entire printing process with your printing service provider. Discover exactly what they need from you. Continue to liaise with your printer while you work on your publication. Ask questions. Get clear answers – and so save money!

2. Establish what type of printing to use – spot color, process color or a mix of the two; how many colors to use; the use of tints or shades; whether to use black-and-white or color photos, etc.

3. Discuss which fonts to use and who will supply them: you or them? Use as few fonts as you need. Use TrueType fonts if possible, as they can be embedded into your publication and your printer can use Publisher's advanced pre-press features.

4. Agree and set deadlines and dates for each stage of printing.

5. Discuss every image that you'll use in your document. For image scans: who does them – you or them? Are there any trapping requirements (page 136)?

6. Decide on the type of the paper to be used in your publication.

7. Discuss options for the folding, trimming and binding of your publication, and delivery of copies to you.

8 Establish in which file format you'll need to deliver your publication: (1) Microsoft Publisher, (2) PostScript, or (3) Portable Document Format (PDF).

Make sure that your printer has in stock all that will be needed to complete your publication, or can access these items as needed, and on time.

9 Determine how to deliver your publication: (1) disk, (2) black-and-white master, copy that you print on your own high resolution desktop printer, or (3) Internet/e-mail electronic file transfer (establish what are the requirements).

10 Taking all of the above into account, establish a budget.

Never set up a color publication that is to be printed commercially, until you have chosen and spoken to the organization who will print your document. Why? You need to make sure you specify in your publication the settings that your printer requires.

Prepare your publication in detail. If you need to make changes after you have handed over your publication for printing, expect to pay significant additional costs. To help avoid those costs, consider the guidelines starting on page 126.

Looking for money-saving tips?

If possible, use spot colors only, and choose from a matching color system such as Pantone. If you use process colors, choose from a matching color chart that your printing service uses, rather than those you see on your computer screen. Your printer can advise what they need.

Use the minimum number of fonts necessary. Avoid using decorative fonts if possible. Print color separations and composite proofs to make sure you get what you expect. Then, if necessary, fix any problems before handing your publication over to your printer. Remove all objects in your publication that are not part of the published document.

Deciding to use spot or process colors

To produce a large quantity of copies of your publication, or to produce a better quality finish than you can achieve from your desktop printer, consider using an outside print shop. You can print a master copy to take to your printer or you can deliver your completed publication on disk in Publisher format; or as a file; or you can send your publication to a print shop using e-mail or the Internet. However, speak to your print shop representatives first to find out exactly what they require from you.

If you're delivering your publication to your print shop on disk, you can copy the Publisher files using the Pack and Go command on the File menu.

Deciding whether to use spot color or process color

If you're using a commercial printer, you can use:

- Spot color: suitable when all colors and shades in a publication are made up from one or two "real" colors. This option provides high-quality output that can be relatively inexpensive.

If your publication is too large to fit onto a single floppy disk, you can use a file compression program. Or consider investing in Zip disks, or other types of portable hard disk solutions. Talk to your print shop representatives about this.

- Process color separations: ideal if your publication contains color photographs or more than two shades of color

If printing your publication to a file, discuss this option in detail with your printing service first. You can discover more information by typing: "Create an EPS file" into the Publisher Help system.

other than black and white. But remember, this option can be particularly expensive.

- Black and white with shades of grey: here printing quality can be excellent and cost can be quite reasonable. Shop around, as prices may vary considerably.

Color Printing dialog box:

Color Printing

Define all colors as:
- ○ Any color (RGB) - Best for desktop printers
- ○ Single color
- ● Spot colors
- ○ Process colors (CMYK)
- ○ Process colors plus spot colors

Tabs: Inks | Colors

In use	● Spot color 1: Black
In use	● Spot color 2: RGB (163, 40, 0)
In use	● Spot color 3: Light Orange
In use	● Spot color 4: RGB (184, 46, 0)
In use	● Spot color 5: RGB (255, 153, 51)
In use	● Spot color 6: RGB (204, 51, 0)
In use	● Spot color 7: RGB (51, 102, 51)

Delete Excess Inks | New Ink...

Reset | OK | Cancel | Help

Working with spot color printing

To add a new spot color, first make sure your publication is set up to use spot colors, as described on this page. In the Color Printing dialog box, click the Inks tab, followed by the New Ink button. Choose the spot color you want from the varieties of options available through the Standard or Custom tabs. Click OK twice.

To convert a publication for printing in spot color

Open the Tools menu and click Commercial Printing Tools, followed by Color Printing. In the Color Printing dialog box (see facing page), under Define all colors as, click Spot colors and Click OK. Publisher lists all the spot colors used in the Inks tab.

To change a spot color

In the Color Printing dialog box referred to above, after you have created spot colors, if you move your mouse pointer over individual inks in the list, and click the down-arrow button on the right side of each ink, Publisher provides access to commands for changing, deleting and duplicating the spot colors listed.

In Publisher, spot colors and spot color inks are not the same. You use spot colors when you design a publication. However, spot color inks are used by a printer to print your publication.

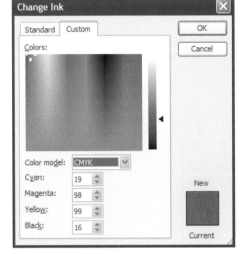

You can replace a spot color with another from several sources: the Pantone Matching System, the Windows color palette, or create a new color using the RGB, HSL or CMYK color models (for outline descriptions, see the first margin tip on this page and pages 130 and 131).

To delete a spot color

Open the Tools menu and click Commercial Printing Tools, followed by Color Printing. Click the Colors tab and scroll down the list of spot colors to find the one you want to delete. Click the down-arrow button on the right side of the spot color you want, then click Delete.

CMYK is the shortened name for a color model used in printing. A wide range of different colors and shades can be created in CMYK, by using varying proportions of cyan (C), magenta (M), yellow (Y) and black (K) inks. Other color models described elsewhere in this chapter are RGB and HSL.

In the Replace Color dialog box, click a color to replace the spot color you are about to delete. Why? In the Colors tab, Publisher lists the spot colors that are in use, so you must install another color before you delete. Click OK to delete your chosen spot color.

Process color printing

To convert a publication for process color printing

Open the Tools menu, click Commercial Printing Tools, followed by Color Printing. Then, continue with the steps below:

1 In the Color Printing dialog box, under Define all colors as, click Process colors (CMYK).

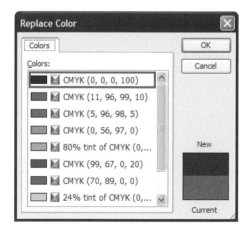

RGB is a color model in Publisher that represents colors in varying percentage proportions of red (R), green (G) and blue (B). White results when all three colors use 100%. Black is created when red, green and blue all use 0%. Other color models described elsewhere in this chapter are CMYK and HSL.

2 If Publisher asks you to confirm, click OK to continue. Publisher then changes all the colors in your current publication to varying proportions of cyan, magenta, yellow and black, as shown listed in the Inks tab.

If you click the Colors tab above, Publisher shows the CMYK values that make up each color.

Also, if you move your mouse pointer over a color and click the down-arrow button on the right side of the color box, Publisher makes available the commands to change or delete (replace) a color.

Using both spot and process colors

Sometimes, a publication requires using a combination of both spot and process colors (see second margin tip). Here's how to convert a publication to use both. First, open the Tools menu and click Commercial Printing Tools, followed by Color Printing. In the Color Printing dialog box, under Define all colors as, click Process colors plus spot colors. If Publisher displays a confirmation box, Click OK to continue. One of three possible outcomes then occurs:

HSL is a color model that is also available in Publisher. HSL determines a color based on Hue (its color), Saturation (how pure the color is) and Luminance (the level of light reflected or absorbed by the color). Other color models described elsewhere in this chapter are CMYK and RGB.

Here's an example when both spot and process color is called for. Imagine you're working on creating a high quality company brochure. Naturally, many companies have a clearly defined brand that must be maintained. If the company marketing department insist that their logo must use specific spot colors, and the brochure must also contain a range of color photos, then a combination of both spot and process color is probably the only solution.

- If your publication was originally designed using CMYK, then in the Inks tab, Publisher lists all the process color inks you originally used. You can also add any new spot color inks using the New Ink button, as described in the first margin tip on page 129.

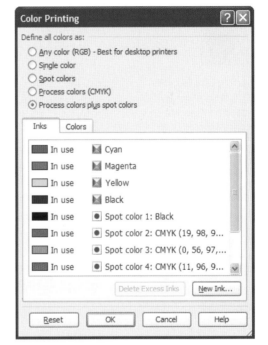

- If your publication was originally designed using several spot colors or a single (spot) color, in the list of inks shown on the Inks tab, Publisher keeps the spot color inks your publication originally used, and also adds the process color inks cyan, magenta, yellow and black.

- If your original publication was designed using RGB colors, in the Inks tab, Publisher converts all the RGB colors your publication originally used to process colors, visible when you click the Colors tab. In the Inks tab, Publisher also adds the process colors cyan, magenta, yellow and black.

Filling an object with Pantone color

Pantone is a popular color-matching standard that covers hundreds of spot and process color (CMYK) inks.

Before applying Pantone color to your publication, discover or determine which type of paper your final publication will be printed on: coated paper, uncoated paper or matte coated paper. Also, if possible, make a note of the Pantone numbers you will be using in your publication. Discuss these two options with your printing service provider if unsure.

You can fill an object with a Pantone process color, or apply Pantone process color to text using similar methods as described on this page for working with Pantone spot color. However, for this option, most importantly, first make sure your publication has been converted to process color printing as described on page 130. Then, under the color options, look for the More Colors button, and find PANTONE under the Color options or Color models listed.

Setup for spot color printing and Pantone color

First, carry out the pre-work outlined in the second margin tip. Next, open the Tools menu and click Commercial Printing tools, followed by Color Printing. Then, click Spot colors.

On the Inks tab, place your mouse pointer on the spot color you want. Click the down-arrow on the right side and click

127	134	1345	141	148
128	135	1355	142	149
129	136	1365	143	150
130	137	1375	144	151
131	138	1385	145	152
132	139	1395	146	153
133	140	1405	147	154

Change, then the Custom tab. Under Color Model, click PANTONE ®, then PANTONE Solid tab.

In Color Type list, click: Coated Paper, Uncoated Paper or Matte Coated Paper. Choose the color you want: click the correct color on the color swatch, or type the Pantone number in the Find Color Name box. Click OK three times to confirm your changes. Now you can apply Pantone colors to objects in your publication as described below.

Apply Pantone color to an object

First, do everything outlined in the previous section above. Then, simply right-click an object in your publication to which you want to apply Pantone color (including outlines and fills), and click Format <object name> command.

For example, if you're changing a shape, you would see Format AutoShape. Next, under the Line and/or Fill options, click the down-arrow button for the Color box, then simply click the color you want. Click OK to confirm you choices.

To change text color to a Pantone color

First, do all the steps listed in "Setup for spot color printing and Pantone color". Next, highlight the text you want to change. Finally, on the Formatting toolbar, click the down-arrow button next to the Font Color button, and click the color you want.

Switching process and spot colors

IMPORTANT: For both tasks outlined on this page, first, make sure you have converted your publication to both process colors and spot colors, as described on page 131.

After, completing the steps in the first paragraph of this page, to convert a process color ink to a spot color ink, perform the following steps:
(1) Click the Colors tab.
(2) Move your mouse pointer to the process color ink you want to convert to spot color.
(3) Click the down-arrow button on the right side of the process color you want, then click Convert to Spot. Publisher then adds the new spot color to the list of inks shown in the Inks tab.

Before performing the steps on this page, read the first margin tip. Next, open the Tools menu and click Commercial Printing Tools, followed by Color Printing. Now continue with the required operation below:

Convert a spot color ink to a process color ink

After, completing the steps above, click the Inks tab. Next, click the down-arrow button on the right side of the spot color you want, then click Convert to Process. Publisher deletes the spot color entry from the list of inks in the Inks tab, and adds the color you just converted to the process color list in the Colors tab.

To convert a process color ink to a spot color ink

This procedure is similar to above, but done in reverse. See the second margin tip for the exact steps to follow.

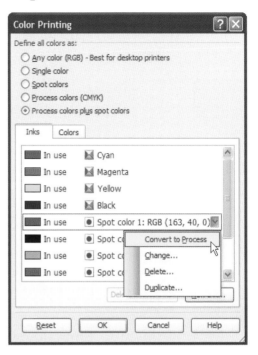

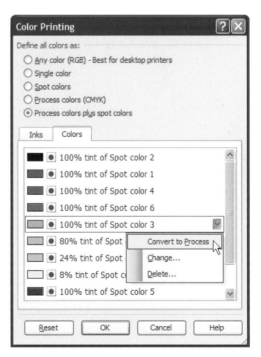

Getting ready for commercial printing

To set up advanced print options

Open the File menu and click Print. Then, under the Printer section, in the Name list, click the printer or imagesetter for which you want to set up advanced print options. Next, choose one of the two following options: (1) Perform the steps to print separations as outlined on the facing page, or (2) choose to print a composite of your publication as described on page 137.

When you use the Pack and Go command, by default Publisher turns on font embedding. However, you can choose not to embed fonts when running the Pack and Go wizard: simply un-check the Embed TrueType Fonts check box.

Now, with the Separations tab displayed in the Advanced Print Settings dialog box, in the Resolution list, click the resolution you want to use to print your publication. Click the Page Settings tab. Choose all the options you want under the sections: Print output, Printer's marks and Bleeds.

Next, click the Graphics and Fonts tab and choose the options you want under the Graphics and Fonts sections. Click OK. Then, to have Publisher store your latest changes as above, click Cancel. Or, if you want to print your publication now, click OK.

Embedding fonts into a publication

Sometimes, you may need to specify a large paper size in File > Page Setup. When you change to a larger paper size in this way, your page in Publisher still remains the same size. Instead, you're just setting a new target page size.

If you're planning to print your publication on another computer, consider embedding the fonts you use into your publication, to ensure you can print or view your publication correctly on another computer. To embed or change font embedding settings, first open the Tools menu and click Commercial Printing Tools followed by Fonts. Choose the options your want. Click OK.

Printing to a file

If your print shop wants you to deliver your publication as a file, here's what you do. After saving your file in Publisher, open the File menu and click Print. In the Print dialog box, click the Print to file check box to insert a tick mark. Make sure that all of your other required printing options and properties have been chosen. Then, click OK.

For lots more information about embedding fonts, see the Publisher online Help under the topic: "About Publisher Font Embedding for Commercial Printing."

In the Print To File dialog box, type a name for your file and choose either the .prn or .eps filename extension. Then locate the folder in which you want to store the PostScript file and double-click it. Finally, click OK. Publisher saves your publication as a file. You can then copy this file to a disk or send it via a modem to your chosen printer.

Printing separations for a publication

When you print a separation, you print one black and white page for each color used. Separations can help a printing service provider evaluate how the colors are arranged in your publication. To print separations of your publication, first, open the File menu and click Print, then continue with the steps below:

To print crop marks, make sure that you're printing on a paper size that is larger than the page size you have set for your publication in Publisher.

To print crop marks, first, see the above margin tip. Then perform the following steps.
(1) Open the File menu and click Print.
(2) Click Advanced Print Settings, then the Page Settings tab.
(3) Under the Printer's marks section, click Crop marks to place a tick mark in the box.
(4) Choose any remaining options you want, then click OK twice to print.
To stop printing crop marks, click the box again in Step 3, to clear the tick mark.

When printing color separations, if you want to include printer's marks, you'll need to print to a paper size that is larger than your publication page size, to ensure that the printer's marks are printed on the paper.

1 Under the Printer section, in the Name box, choose the printer you want.

2 Click Advanced Print Settings, followed by the Separations tab.

3 In the Output category, click the drop-down arrow button and then click Separations.

4 In the These plates category, click the drop-down arrow button to display the list of options. Then perform Step 5, Step 6 or Step 7.

5 To set Publisher to print a spot color or process color plate (separation) to represent every ink you set up in the Tools menu > Commercial Printing Tools > Color Printing, click All defined links.

6 To tell Publisher to print a spot color or process color plate (separation) for every ink used in the publication, click Used inks only.

7 To have Publisher to convert all spot colors you have set up, to process colors, click Convert spot to process.

8 If you want to stop Publisher printing separations for any unused process colors, click Don't print blank plates, to place a tick mark in the box.

9 Choose any remaining options you want in the other two tabs: Page Settings and Graphics and Fonts, and click OK.

10 Click OK again to print your separations.

About bleeds and trapping values

In commercial color printing, while a publication is being printed, the paper or printing plates can shift or stretch slightly and misregistration of the inks can occur. However, Publisher allows you to compensate for these effects by using two key techniques: trapping and overprinting (see adjacent margin tips for more information).

When you start a new publication, by default, Publisher does not apply any trapping. If you decide to use trapping, you can use the default settings suggested by Publisher or you can apply your own. Publisher follows its own set of sophisticated rules to determine trapping values and has a powerful range of trapping options. You can view details by entering "About trapping in Publisher" into the Help task pane search box, then click the search button. To apply automatic trapping, perform the steps below:

1 Open the Tools menu and click Commercial Printing Tools, followed by Registration Settings, then Publication.

2 Click the Automatic trapping check box to add a tick mark.

3 Click the OK button to confirm your changes.

4 When trapping is turned on, Publisher traps the entire publication.

Publication Registration Settings

Trapping settings
- ☑ Automatic trapping   [Thresholds...]
- Width: 0.25pt
- Indeterminate: 0.25pt
- ☐ Only allow spread traps on text glyphs

Spot color options

Spot Colors	Luminance

Luminance:
☑ Trap white as a color

Overprinting Settings
- ☑ Text below: 24pt   ☑ Lines
- Overprint threshold: 95   ☐ Fills
                               ☑ Imported pictures

[Reset All]   [OK]   [Cancel]   [Help]

Creating a composite of a publication

If your commercial printing service provider asks for a composite of your publication, first, open the File menu and click Print. Then follow the steps below:

When starting to send a publication by e-mail, here's a quick way to determine how your publication will be received by your intended recipient later. Simply, send a copy of the e-mail to yourself first. Examine the publication you sent. If all is well, you can send to your recipient with confidence.

1 Click Advanced Print Settings.

2 With the Separations tab displayed, in the Output list of options, choose the option you want as described in Step 3, Step 4 and Step 5.

3 If you want to print a composite to a black-and-white printer, click Composite Grayscale.

4 If you want to print a composite to a process color printer or proofing tool, click Composite CMYK. Optionally, choose any remaining setting on the Page Settings tab and Graphics and Fonts tab.

5 If you want to print a composite to a desktop color printer, click Composite RGB.

6 Click OK twice to print your composite.

When sending a Publisher print publication by e-mail, remember most print documents are designed for printed page sizes rather than e-mail windows, so you may get some layout problems. One remedy to consider is to choose a publication type that is especially designed for e-mail format. For more information, see the templates in Web Sites and E-mail in the New Publication task pane.

To save a composite as a CMYK PostScript file

Perform the following steps. (1) Open the File menu and click Save As. (2) In the File name box, type a name for your file – don't include a filename extension.

(3) In the Save as type list, click PostScript. Publisher then inserts the .ps filename extension at the end of your filename in Step 2 above. (4) Click Save.

(5) Under the Printer section, in the Name list, click the PostScript color printer you want. (6) Click Advanced Print Settings, then the Separations tab.

(7) In the Output section, click Composite CMYK from the drop-down list. (8) Choose any additional settings you want on the Page Settings tab and the Graphics and Fonts tab, then click OK.

(9) Back in the Save As PostScript File dialog box, click the Save button to save your CMYK composite.

You can send a publication to anyone in three ways: (1) on disk (using Pack and Go), (2) provide a master copy (your own high resolution printout), or (3) send all files using the Internet or e-mail.

Monochrome or single color printing

To print your publication designed for a single spot color, first, perform the following steps.

First, open the Tools menu and click the Commercial Printing Tools command.

Next, click the Color Printing command. In the Color Printing dialog box, click Single color.

Publisher then changes all colors in the publication to tints based on a single color.

As a baseline from which to complete the action, the color Publisher chooses as the initial default, is usually the darkest color in your publication.

However, you can change the default color at any time. See page 129 for details.

To view the range of tints Publisher creates, click the Colors tab.

Publisher can embed TrueType fonts in the current publication when the fonts are not already installed in Windows and providing the fonts you use allow embedding. However, Publisher embeds only TrueType fonts and all the fonts included with Publisher that automatically have full embedding rights.

Color Printing

Define all colors as:

- Any color (RGB) - Best for desktop printers
- Single color
- Spot colors
- Process colors (CMYK)
- Process colors plus spot colors

Inks | Colors

In use ● Spot color 1: CMYK (0, 0, 0, 1...

Delete Excess Inks | New Ink...

Reset | OK | Cancel | Help

Color Printing

Define all colors as:

- Any color (RGB) - Best for desktop printers
- Single color
- Spot colors
- Process colors (CMYK)
- Process colors plus spot colors

Inks | Colors

● 100% tint of Spot color 1
● 76% tint of Spot color 1
● 73% tint of Spot color 1
● 72% tint of Spot color 1
● 69% tint of Spot color 1
● 45% tint of Spot color 1
● 36% tint of Spot color 1
● 20% tint of Spot color 1
● 0% tint of Spot color 1

Reset | OK | Cancel | Help

Using the Pack and Go wizard

Pack and Go gathers together a publication with all its linked files and packs everything into a single file. The file provides an easy way to copy a Publisher publication to another computer, or to present it to your commercial printing service for final printing. If after packing a file, you need to make some quick changes to the original file, remember to run Pack and Go again, to ensure that the packed file contains the latest version. Pack and Go has two variations: one for creating files for computer-to-computer sharing, and another tailored to delivering a publication to a commercial printer.

If you want to send several publications using Pack and Go, first save each publication into a separate folder. Otherwise, each Pack and Go package will overwrite the previously packed publication.

Using Pack and Go to share a publication with another computer

This version of Pack and Go embeds any TrueType fonts used, bundles any linked graphics within your publication, and provides an option to split the final file across several storage disks. When finished, Pack and Go generates a file called Packed01.puz, saves it along with another separate file called unpack.exe, and a readme.txt file, to a location you choose. Unpack.exe is used to unpack the packed publication when ready, and after unpacking, adds the .png filename extension to the unpacked filename

To unpack a packed file, simply double-click Unpack.exe, then type in or browse to the location where you want to unpack your file. Then click OK to start unpacking.

Using Pack and Go to send a publication to a commercial printer

This version of Pack and Go will create linked graphics from any graphics that were originally embedded and add these linked graphics to the final packed publication.

Also, if any problems are found with linked graphics, Pack and Go lists the problem graphics. Pack and Go also automatically embeds any TrueType fonts that are used. If any fonts cannot be embedded, Pack and Go identifies and lists those fonts. Before completing, the wizard prompts you to choose whether you want to print a composite, a separation draft, or both. Finally, there's an option that enables you to share the final packed file across several disks.

Any fonts that were originally embedded in a packed publication, will still be available once the publication is unpacked on a different computer. However, the embedded fonts cannot be used like normal Windows' fonts. Embedded fonts are only visible in the publication into which they were embedded.

To pack a file for commercial printing, first open the File menu, click Pack and Go, followed by Take to Commercial Printing Service. Then follow the guidelines in the wizard to save your packed file.

Sending your publication by e-mail

An ideal tool to use if you want to pass on or obtain important information quickly, especially if both parties are using faster Internet connections, e.g. a cable modem or ASDL modem. If you have Office Outlook 2003 or Outlook Express (v5.0 and later) installed as your default e-mail application, you can send a publication by e-mail as: (1) an entire publication in an e-mail message, (2) part of a publication as an e-mail message, or (3) as an e-mail attachment.

To send a publication as an attachment

For this option, your recipient must have Microsoft Publisher 2002, or a later version, installed on their computer. To send a Publisher file as an attachment to an e-mail, first make sure that you've saved your publication. Then, open the File menu and click Send E-Mail, followed by Send Publication as Attachment. Publisher opens a new window in your default e-mail program. In the To box, type or choose the e-mail address of your recipient. Include any additional information you want in the Subject box and message body area, then click Send.

To send the currently displayed page of a publication as an e-mail message

For this option, in order to view the e-mail message, your recipient does not need to have Office Publisher 2003 installed. However, they must have Microsoft Office Outlook 2003 or Microsoft Outlook Express (v5.0 or later) installed on the PC they're using to receive your publication. Open the File menu, click Send E-Mail, followed by Send This Page as Message. Publisher adds e-mail boxes and an e-mail toolbar into the main Publisher window. Type or choose the e-mail address of your recipient, and include any other additional information you want in the Subject box. Then click the Send button on the e-mail toolbar.

To preview the current page before sending by e-mail

For this option, you must have Microsoft Office Outlook 2003 or Microsoft Outlook Express (v5.0 or later) installed on the PC you're using to preview the publication you want to send.

Open the File menu, click Send E-Mail, followed by E-Mail Preview. Publisher then opens your default browser and displays the page as viewed in an e-mail message.

Creating web pages in Publisher

Publisher is a deceptively powerful web design program. In this and several subsequent chapters, we explore web mode and how to create smart websites in Publisher.

Covers

Chapter Twelve

Website basics

The Internet and the web defined

For many businesses, information is the new currency, and the web now offers one of the most powerful ways in which to quickly gain access to the most up-to-date information.

While the Internet is the world's largest network of connected computers, the World Wide Web (WWW) – nowadays usually shortened to just the web – provides an easy and colorful way to use and move around the Internet.

Today, anyone with access to a PC and an Internet connection, can advertise or market themselves and their products to the world, on the web and at low cost. If you want to build up *and* maintain the number of visitors, one of the most important points to remember is to provide a strong reason for people to visit your website: offer web content that is unique, valuable, attractive and interesting.

For businesses, organizations and clubs

If you publish material on the web that you don't own, ensure that you have copyright or permission to do so, to avoid possible costly litigation.

A carefully designed and compelling website can provide a powerful way in which to market to new prospects, make new customers and keep in contact with existing customers, members and staff. Once your clients have recorded or

"bookmarked" your website, you can easily keep in contact with them using web promotions, features, special offers and so on.

For individuals

With Publisher, you can quickly create interesting, engaging single- or multi-page web designs, tailored for business, community or personal use.

You can set up your own simple "Home Page" as a fun way to contact others who share your interests. Or you can advertise your skills and display your résumé (CV) to potential employers. You can establish a web page for fun and to entertain your

friends and colleagues. Or, you may want to enhance your career, impress your boss or provide an all-singing, all-dancing résumé-oriented website, ready for those all-important job interviews.

Planning your website

For businesses, effective website design is crucial. *For a business-oriented website, every single component that goes to make up the site must contribute in some way to sales.* Through applying a little thought and consideration, you can create an effective, compelling website that engages your prospect, persuades, or urges your customer to buy.

On your Home or Index page, tell your visitors to bookmark the page as a Favorite, so that they can always find your site again easily.

Finding web images and special graphics

To assist you in choosing graphics to include on your web pages, Microsoft has developed hundreds of pictures in the Clip Gallery and on Microsoft Office Online, which are especially "tuned" for use in web pages. Some are animated to provide an added element of interest to your web pages. Sound clips too are available and can provide the finishing touch to help create a really stunning presentation.

Keep a backup copy of your website files, before changing the original version. You can use the Save with Backup option on the Save button, in the Save As dialog box.

To see a range of e-mail buttons, Navigation bars and page dividers, click the Design Gallery Object button on the Objects toolbar. You can view these objects organized in categories or as design set elements. To learn more about the Design Gallery, see Chapter 7.

Your website design: start-off questions to consider

When considering how to design your website, with paper and pen in hand, ask yourself some basic questions: who, what, where, when, how and why. Who is the website for? What shall I include? Where am I going to host my website? When do I need it to be ready? How am I going to structure my website? Why do I want a website? And so on. This initial exercise can give you a better feel for your website project. For a business-oriented website, four especially important questions to answer are:

Consider how long your web pages take to load. Even though more people today may have fast "always on" Internet connections, many people around the world are still using slow connections or paying by-the-minute for Internet access.

- Who is my website really for? Define your visitors.

- What is the most important goal that I want to achieve with my new website?

- What kind of look and feel or impression do I want to put over? Serious? Light and funny? News-driven? Edgy? Etc.

- How do I get my website visitors to return to my website regularly? Consider how to make your website "sticky".

Using a wizard to create your website

The quickest way to create a website in Publisher is to use a wizard and let Publisher do most of the initial design work for you. When you start a website wizard, Publisher asks you some basic questions about what kind of website you want to create, and prompts you for details you want entered. After the wizard has done its work, you can modify the design to include the content you want.

To start a website wizard, first, open the File menu and click New. In the New Publication task pane, click Web Sites and E-Mail, then click Web Sites. Publisher provides four wizard options.

To create a custom website, click Easy web Site Builder. To create a three-page website containing a Home page, an About Us page and a Contact Us page, click 3-Page Web Site. To create a sales website with multiple sales pages, click Product Sales. To create a website tailored for professional services, click Professional Services.

Once, you've made your choice in the previous paragraph, in the right pane of the New Publication wizard, click the website design you want. Publisher creates your website template. Double-click each item and replace with your own content. Develop your website further as desired. Save your new website.

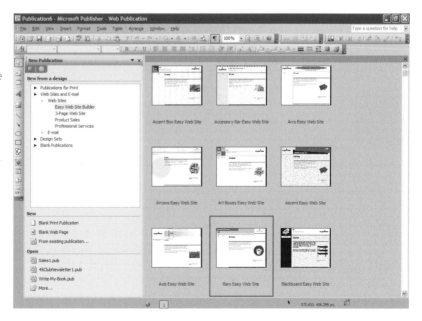

Creating web pages your way

Even though Publisher provides a wide range of predesigned web page templates, you may prefer to create your own masterpiece from scratch. Follow the steps below.

You can learn more about how to avoid web page design pitfalls from the international best-seller, Web Page Design in easy steps, also from this series.

1 Open the File menu, and click New.

2 In the New Publication task pane, under New, click Blank web page. Publisher shows the No Design option selected.

3 (Optional) In the task pane, you also have easy access to all the key commands in: Web Site Options, Page Content, Publication Designs, Color Schemes, and Font Schemes.

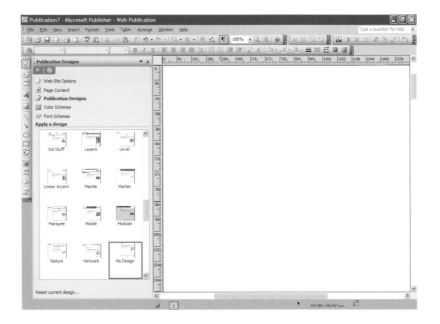

If you're creating an entirely new web page, simply add the desired text, graphics, tables, WordArt or any other objects just as you would with any other Publisher document. However, if you're adding web-related items like hyperlinks (page 153), and web page backgrounds and textures, a different approach is needed. Read the remaining pages in this chapter to master the basics about how to create smart web pages in Publisher.

Use existing web pages to create a site

HyperText Markup Language (HTML) is one way in which web pages can be created today. When you create a website in Publisher and publish it to the Web, Publisher converts your web publication into a version of HTML.

If you don't want to use a Publisher wizard, or start from scratch, you can create a website based on an existing HTML file (see first margin tip stipulations though). First, open the File menu and click Open, then perform the steps below.

You must have permission from the copyright owner, or have a license to use an existing HTML file, before you can copy or modify it. For example, your existing HTML file may come in the form of a commercial web page template design which you may purchase on the web. Thousands of web design templates are now available.

To see some examples of commercial web page design templates, first connect to the Internet and open your web browser. Next, click the Search button and type "web design templates" (without the quotes) into the Search box, then press Enter.

1 In the Open Publication dialog box, in the Look in list, move to the drive, folder, Internet or web location where the HTML file you want to use is located.

2 Select the HTML folder containing the file you want.

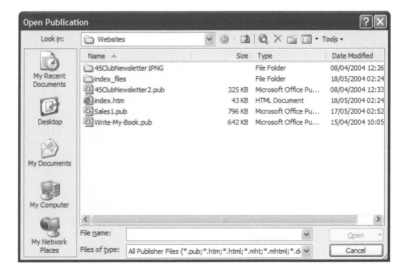

3 Click the HTML web page you want to select it. Then click the Open button.

Web fonts and Publisher font schemes

Web fonts

The font styles you use in a web publication can affect how easy or difficult your text content is to read. Publisher makes available specific fonts that have been designed for use in web publications and to help provide easy reading on a computer screen.

To have Publisher make available only web fonts, first open the Format menu and click Font. Then, in the Font dialog box, click Show only web fonts. Then click OK to confirm you change.

Publisher's web fonts are: Arial, Arial Black, Comic Sans MS, Courier New, Georgia, Impact, Symbol, Times New Roman, Trebuchet, Verdana and Wingdings.

Publisher's web font schemes

Web font schemes are pre-arranged sets of fonts in Publisher that complement each other.

The web font schemes are: Archival, Basis, Binary, Casual, Data, Foundation, Impact, Online, Versatile and Virtual.

Publisher provides two ways to ensure that text can look the same in different web browsers: (1) use only web fonts (see above), or (2) convert your text block to one of the following picture formats: GIF, JPEG or PNG.

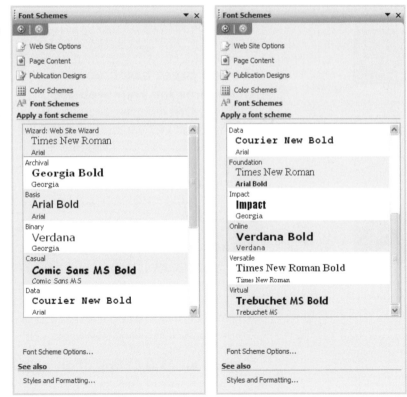

Adding, copying and deleting pages

To add a new web page

The page sorter is the group of small page-shaped icons situated in the lower left corner of the screen to represent the pages in your publication. You can right-click on a page icon to access further page commands.

Open the Insert menu, then click Page. In the Insert Web Page dialog box, explore the options under Select a page type. Options with a right-pointing triangle, contain more options: click to view. Click the More button to get access to more page options (see illustration below). Make your choices and click OK.

To add pages based on your main aims for your website

To quickly identify a page in your website, move your mouse pointer over the icons in page sorter (referred to above). Publisher displays a ScreenTip identifying each page.

Make sure the task pane is visible. If not, open the View menu and click Task Pane. Choose the Web Site Options task pane, then click Add functionality, to display the Easy Web Site Builder dialog box. Make your choices and click OK.

To add a new blank page

To delete a page, on the page sorter, right-click on the page you want to delete. Then, from the floating menu, click Delete Page.

With your mouse pointer on the page sorter at the bottom of the screen, right-click on the page where you want to insert a new blank page. From the floating menu, click Insert Page. Publisher displays the Insert Web Page dialog box (see top illustration). Under the Select a page type listing, click Blank, then OK.

To add an exact copy of an existing web page

On the page sorter (see above), right-click on the page you want to copy. From the floating menu, click the Duplicate Page command.

Feeding search engines and directories

Before publishing your website to the web, there are some simple steps you should take to help make your website more accessible in the Internet search engines and web directories. A web page title is what appears in your web browser Title bar. The title is especially important as it is used in search engine listings, helps rank a web page and can appear in web searches.

The Web browser Title bar appears at the top of your web browser window and usually contains the Title of the web page being viewed.

To give a title and a filename to a web page

Move to the web page to which you want to give a title. Then, open the Tools menu and click Web Page Options.

If you type a filename, Publisher will not accept spaces or special characters. Use letters or numbers only.

In the Web Page Options dialog box, click in the Page title box and type the title

Make a list of keywords that describe your website. Consider variations in spelling – for example: ize and ise – even common spelling mistakes. Also, include plural variations, as these can also cover singular searches as well. Example: "books" also includes "book". Include brief descriptions; example: fiction books, short stories, and so on.

Web Page Options

Page title: Product Detail

☑ Add hyperlink to new navigation bars that are added to this publication.

Publish to the Web

File name: _____ .htm

By default, Publisher creates a file name when you publish your Web site. If you want to specify the file name, type the file name here. Do not use spaces or special characters.

Search engine information

Type the page title, description, and keywords that best describe your Web site. This information is used by search engines to generate search results.

Description: Describe what your website does here

Keywords: add single words and phrases that describe your website here

Background sound

File name: _____ Browse...

○ Loop forever   ⦿ Loop   1 ⏶ time(s)

Web Site Options...   OK   Cancel   Help

you want to use for your web page. In the Publish to the Web box, you can also type a filename for your web page (see second margin tip). Publisher uses filenames to name each page when you publish your website. Click OK to finish.

About keywords (META tags)

Keywords, otherwise known as META tags, help provide information about your website to a search engine. Publisher uses two main META tags: keywords and description. Although you can include META keywords on every page that makes up your website, the most important page is the Home/Index page.

In the Web Page Options dialog box, under Search engine information, in the Description box, type a brief sentence that describes the purpose of your website. You are limited to 256 characters. In the Keywords box, you can type the kinds of words a visitor might use to search for your website. Separate you keywords and key phrases by commas. You are limited to 256 characters.

Establishing your web page background

To set a different background color or texture for a website

Complementary colors and textures can create depth to a web page and stimulate added interest in your website as a whole. Publisher provides a range of textures and colors which you can apply to your web pages.

To add or change a web page background color or texture, first open the Format menu and click the Background command. Publisher displays the Background task pane. Then carry out the steps below.

Make sure there is sufficient color contrast between text and a web page background. If the background color/texture is too strong, reading web text may be difficult for your visitor.

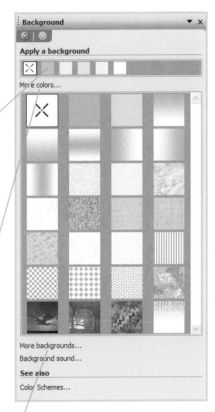

1 To choose a background color, click the new background color you want.

2 Click more colors if you want to see a wider range of colors, then click the color you want.

3 Click OK.

4 Click the new color you want in the now updated task pane.

To choose a background that uses a gradient, texture, pattern, picture or tint, click More backgrounds, then choose the options you want. Click OK to apply your new choices. Think carefully before choosing a picture for a background. Why? If the file size is larger than about 20 kilobytes, your web pages may take too long to download in a visitor's web browser.

Setting web page width

To change the width of a web page, first open the File menu and click Page Setup. Then, continue with the steps below.

1 Click the Layout tab.

2 Under the Publication type list, select Web page.

In Step 3, Narrow is designed for low resolution screens and is not used so often today. Computer screens have become larger with better definition in recent years. Normally, Standard is the ideal setting for today's high resolution screens.

3 Under Page size click either Narrow (640 pixels wide by 480 pixels high) or select Standard (800 pixels wide by 600 pixels high). See first margin tip.

4 Click OK to apply the new web page size.

A pixel is a tiny dot of light, and is a standard unit of measurement used to draw an image of a set size on a screen. The pixel is the default measurement unit for web pages. You may see pixels written as px.

Page Setup

Layout | Printer and Paper

Publication type
- Custom
- Web page

Page size
- Narrow (640x480 display)
- Standard (800x600 display)

Width: 760px

Preview

Fits in higher-resolution display without horizontal scrolling.

Convert to print publication

Your publication is optimized for display on the Web. If you plan to print your publication, you should convert it to a Publisher print publication.

[Convert to Print Publication...]

[OK] [Cancel] [Help]

To set a custom web page size

Display the Page Set up dialog box as outlined above, then perform the steps below.

1 Under Publication type, click Custom.

2 In the Width and Height boxes, type the values you want and click OK.

Adding a separate **HTML** code block

In HTML, you can insert blocks of code that perform specific functions. For example you may want to add a line of horizontally scrolling text across a web page.

To place an HTML code fragment on a web page

First, go to where you have your HTML code fragment, select it and copy to the Windows Clipboard. Open the Insert menu and click HTML Code Fragment. Then continue with the remaining steps below.

If when you preview your web page, the HTML code fragment you're using does not display or behave as you would expect, check the following. The code fragment could be faulty, incompatible with your web browser, or overlapping another object in Publisher. Drag clear of overlapping objects, then preview your page again.

1 In the Edit HTML Code Fragment dialog box, type or paste your HTML code over the entire placeholder text, deleting the placeholder, and click OK.

2 On the web page, Publisher places your pasted HTML code fragment into a text box frame.

External code fragments can present a security risk. Only consider using code fragments from trusted sources. Publisher does not verify that your code fragment is safe to use. Also, make sure that you have permission to use the code fragment.

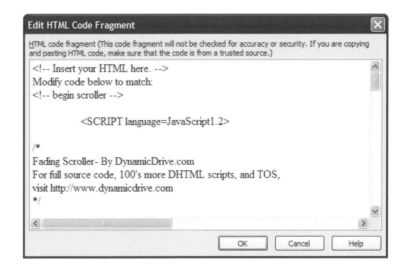

3 Save your updated web page.

4 To view the effect of your HTML code fragment, preview or publish your page and view it in a web browser.

Working with hyperlinks

What is a hyperlink?

A hyperlink is a connection between one item and another item in the same document, to another web document, or to another part of the web.

What does a hyperlink look like?

A hyperlink is like a key providing access to another part of the web. When you click on a hyperlink, you immediately move to where the link is pointing.

A hyperlink can be made up of text, a picture, or part of a picture. Most often, the destination item to which a hyperlink points may be another web page, or it can be a picture, an e-mail address or a software program (like media player for example).

In a web browser, if you place your mouse pointer on a hyperlink, the mouse pointer changes to a pointing finger/hand symbol. After a visitor clicks a hyperlink, Windows usually displays the destination of the hyperlink in the web browser window URL address box, although sometimes, a new window may be opened.

More about the Uniform Resource Locator (URL)

Here's a quick way to check if an object or a section of text is a hyperlink and if so, where the hyperlink points to. Simply place the mouse pointer on top of the text or object you want to check. Publisher then displays a ScreenTip.

When you create a hyperlink to another web page, file or program, Publisher uses a URL. An example URL or web address is: http://www.ineasysteps.com/books.html or: file://JohnSmith/MyDocuments/myfile.htm

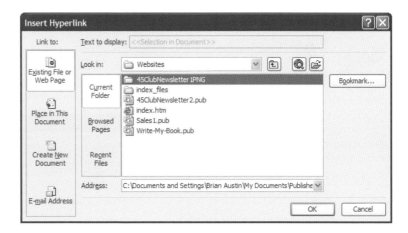

If you prefer, instead of using the Hyperlink command in the Insert menu, you can click the Insert Hyperlink button on the Standard toolbar.

To create or change a hyperlink to a page or file

First, highlight the text or select the picture that you want to convert to a hyperlink. Next, open the Insert menu and click Hyperlink. Under the Link to section (see illustration above), click Existing File or Web Page.

Under Look in, to select a file you want in My Documents, click Current Folder. Then click the file you want, followed by OK. To select a web page you recently viewed, click Browsed Pages. Then click the web page you want, followed by OK. To select a file that you have recently been working with, click Recent Files. Then click the file you want, followed by OK.

Text hyperlinks are easily spotted. Publisher displays each hyperlink in a different color to the rest of your text, or the hyperlink is shown underlined.

To create or change a hyperlink to another page in the current website

First, highlight the text or select the picture that you want to convert to a hyperlink. Next, open the Insert menu and click Hyperlink. Then, under the Link to section (see above), click Place in This Document. Select the page you want and click OK.

If desired, an entire picture can be split up into multiple hyperlinks that link to different destinations. This kind of hyperlink is called an imagemap. Each individual hyperlink part of an image is called a hot spot.

To create a hyperlink to a new web page document

First, highlight the text or select the picture that you want to convert to a hyperlink. Next, open the Insert menu and click Hyperlink. Under the Link to section, click Create New Document (see lower illustration on facing page).

To remove a hyperlink, first select the hyperlink you want to remove. Next, open the Insert menu and click Insert Hyperlink. Then click the Remove Link button. To remove a hyperlink including its text, select the hyperlink you want and press Delete.

If you want to create a new document, in the Name of new document box, type the path and the name you want to use for the new document. Or if you want to change an existing document, click the Change button to move to a location and change an existing web page. Under When to edit, select either Edit the new document later, or Edit the new document now. Click OK.

To change the wording used in hyperlinked text, first select the text you want to change. Then, simply type the new text you want inside the area you just highlighted.

To create or change an e-mail hyperlink

First, select the text or picture you want to convert into an e-mail link. Next, open the Insert menu and click Hyperlink. Under the Link to section, click E-mail Address. Type the e-mail address into the E-mail address box, or select an e-mail address from the list of Recently used e-mail addresses. Click OK.

Absolute and relative hyperlinks explained

Essentially, an absolute hyperlink links to a full URL or web address. Example: http://www.ineasysteps.com/books.html. A relative hyperlink misses off the first part of the URL. For example: /books.html or just books.html. When you create hyperlinks in Publisher, usually the hyperlinks between a website's own pages use relative hyperlinking.

Introduction to web graphics

Consider the following tips when working with graphics for use on a website:

Graphic images that come with Publisher for use in websites, are formatted and optimized especially for downloading quickly on the web: an important feature!

- always make sure you have permission from the copyright holder, to use any graphics that you place on your web pages

- normally, use the Graphics Interchange Format (GIF) for simple graphics like logos, large sweeps of a single color, clip art and simple drawings. Filenames end in .gif. This format can also show basic animations in the form of animated GIFs

Alternative or ALT text is a brief text label description given to a picture. Adding ALT text is useful for a variety of reasons, including: helping physically challenged visitors and improving ranking in search engines. See next tip.

- for photos and scanned images, usually, you'll want to use Joint Photographic Experts Group (JPEG) format. Filenames usually end in .jpg

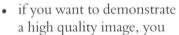

- if you want to demonstrate a high quality image, you may opt for Portable Network Graphics (PNG) format, which ends in .png. This format can be suitable for a wide range of image types, but some web browsers may not support it. In most instances, GIF and JPEG format should be adequate

- try to use each image more than once throughout your website. For example, the same image for a company logo could be used on every page in the website

To insert alternative text, select the first image to which you want to add ALT text. Open the Format menu and click Picture, followed by the Web tab. In the Alternative text box, type the text you want to apply to the selected image, and click OK. Repeat for all images in your website. See previous tip.

- keep the file size of all graphics as low as possible. That means, your images should be optimized for web viewing. Publisher provides access to many optimized images in the Clip Gallery and from Microsoft Office Online

- ideally, keep the total graphics file size per page to under about 50 kilobytes, to speed up total download time

- if you want to display larger images, one option is to provide a small thumbnail image, that is hyperlinked to another web page that contains the full size image. Thumbnail images are outlined later in this chapter

Including animated graphics

Animated graphics can provide an element of action or excitement to a web page. An animated graphic can enhance interest in a web page and provide an effective eye-catching focus.

They come in several forms but the two most popular are animated GIFs and Flash. Flash animation is beyond the scope of this book, but Publisher does include access to a range of animated GIFs. So just what is an animated GIF? Answer: typically, a smaller icon-type image that appears to contain some moving components.

To include an animated picture in your web page

Open the Insert menu, click Picture, then From File. Continue with the steps below:

| In the Insert Picture dialog box, move to the folder where your animated picture is located, then click the picture you want to select it.

2 Click the Insert button.

In the Microsoft Internet Explorer web browser, usually, you can right-click over an animated picture to display a menu, then choose the Save (Picture) As command to save it as a file. Many animations are copyrighted so check if you have legal permission to do this first.

When you publish a website, Publisher converts any rotated text, BorderArt, and gradient text fills used in text boxes, to graphics. Remember, in a web page, graphics do not load as quickly as "pure" text.

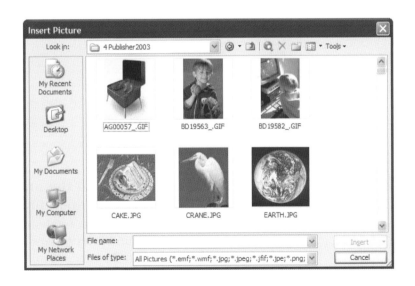

Once the animation is placed on the page, you can resize or move it just like any other object. You won't see the animation in Publisher. To view your animated picture, preview your website in your web browser.

Creating thumbnail graphics

To create a thumbnail image

Click the image from which you want to create a thumbnail. Open the Edit menu and click Copy, then Paste. Publisher places two identical images almost on top of each other. Right-click on the top image, then click Format Picture, followed by the Size tab. Under the Scale section, select Lock aspect ratio. Click OK. Now place the mouse pointer on one of the corner adjust handles. When you see the Resize pointer, press and hold down Shift, then drag the adjust handle to reduce the size of the image to about a 1 inch square or 2.5 cm square. Drag your new thumbnail where you want, or save the thumbnail image for later use.

Preview your web page containing the thumbnail image. Then, click the thumbnail image to verify that your web browser displays the page containing the full size image.

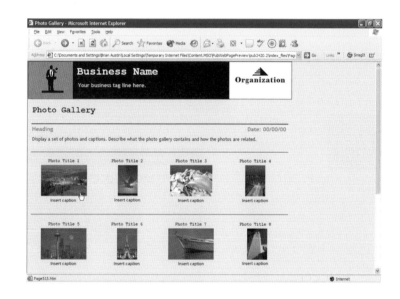

To link a thumbnail to the original size image

Place the thumbnail image you want to use onto a web page where you want and Save the page. Go to where the original size image is located, then click to select the full size image. Open the Edit menu and click Cut. Now move to or create the web page where the original size image is to be placed, then Paste the image onto the page. Drag and position the pasted image where you want. Save the page if necessary. Move back to the web page that contains the thumbnail image. Click your thumbnail image, then open the Insert menu and click Hyperlink. Create a hyperlink to the page that contains the full size image. Save your page.

Using web page navigation bars

A navigation bar is a group of related hyperlinks that enable a visitor to easily move around a website, or link to external web pages. Usually, the same navigation bar is placed in the same position somewhere on all pages in a website.

You can include different types of navigation bar on a page. For example, you may want to use a set of buttons towards the top of a web page, and also include the equivalent hyperlinks in pure text form at the bottom of web pages.

A navigation bar can be made up of hyperlinked buttons or text links. Navigation bars can help visitors quickly establish where they are in a website (see first margin tip). A navigation bar can be vertical or horizontal and can be further formatted in a variety of ways. One of the most useful features of a navigation bar, is that you can set it to display the button that shows the currently selected page differently in some way to the other buttons.

To create a navigation bar

Open the Insert menu, click Navigation Bar, followed by New. Publisher displays the Design Gallery dialog box. On the Objects by Category tab, click the navigation bar design style you want in the right-side pane. Click the Insert Object button.

Commands available to work with navigation bars are only available for web publications.

Publisher displays the Create New Navigation Bar dialog box, as shown overleaf. In the Name box, type a name for your new navigation bar. Under Insert options and Automatic update, choose the options you want. Click OK.

Back on your web page, drag your new navigation bar to the position you want, save the publication and test using the Web Page Preview button on the Standard toolbar

Create New Navigation Bar

Name:
Navigation Bar 1

Insert options
⊙ Insert on every page
○ Insert on this page only

Automatic update
☑ Update this navigation bar with links to existing pages in this publication.

[OK] [Cancel] [Help]

To change a navigation bar

Select the navigation bar, then open the Format menu and click Navigation Bar Properties. Using the commands in the General and Style tabs, you can change the look, modify the links and style used, and specify horizontal or vertical, small or large buttons or text only, number of links used, navigation bar alignment, colors and fonts used, and so on.

To set a navigation bar button to show the selected page differently from other buttons

Select the navigation bar you want. Then open the Format menu, click Navigation Bar Properties, followed by the Style tab.

Select the check box Show selected state to tick mark the box.

To have Publisher display all buttons on the navigation bar to look the same for all web pages in the current website, clear the tick mark from this check box. Click OK to finish.

To delete a navigation bar, first click the navigation bar you want to delete. Publisher shows the selected object with selection handles around its outline. Open the Edit menu and click Delete Object. If you have the same navigation bar on other pages, repeat the previous steps to delete the navigation bar from all the pages you want.

Navigation Bar Properties

General | Style

Apply a design:
⊙ Small buttons ○ Large buttons ○ Text only

Page Title   Ambient

Page Title   Baseline

Page Title   Bracket

☑ Show selected state

Orientation and alignment
⊙ Vertical (column of hyperlinks)
○ Horizontal (row of hyperlinks)
Maximum number of hyperlinks across: 4

Hyperlink alignment: Left

[OK] [Cancel] [Help]

Adding a sound clip to a web page

You can include a background sound so that when visitors view your page, the desired sound clip plays automatically.

Sound components can be made up of music, speech, other miscellaneous sounds or a combination of any of these.

First, move to the web page on to which you want to add a background sound. Then, open the Tools menu, and click Web Page Options. Now continue with the steps below.

When you add a background sound to a web page, the sound won't play when you view the web page in Publisher. To hear the sound, view the web page in a web browser (providing your PC hardware supports sound).

Web Page Options

Page title: About Us

☑ Add hyperlink to new navigation bars that are added to this publication.

Publish to the Web

File name: _____ .htm

By default, Publisher creates a file name when you publish your Web site. If you want to specify the file name, type the file name here. Do not use spaces or special characters.

Search engine information

Type the page title, description, and keywords that best describe your Web site. This information is used by search engines to generate search results.

Description: _____

Keywords: _____

Background sound

File name: C:\Program Files\Microsoft Office\CLIPART\PUB([Browse...]

○ Loop forever ◉ Loop 1 time(s)

[Web Site Options...] [OK] [Cancel] [Help]

Consider carefully whether to include a sound clip in a web page. Some visitors may not share your taste and can become irritated. Remember, this sound clip will play at least once (depending on how many loops you choose) every time the web page displays.

1 Under Background sound, in the File name box, type the path to the sound file you want. Or do Step 2 instead.

2 Click Browse, then select a sound file, and click Open, to have Publisher enter the path for you in the File name box.

3 Decide whether you want the sound clip to play continuously while the web page is being viewed. If yes, click Loop forever. If no, go to Step 4.

4 To have the sound clip play a set number of times, click Loop and select the number of loops you want .

5 Click OK.

6 Now view your web page in a compatible web browser to hear the sound clip.

Saving your site in Publisher format

After you have created your website in Publisher – and frequently during your edits – open the File menu and click Save or Save As.

If it is the first time you have saved this file, Publisher displays the Save As dialog box, in which you choose a location to save your website and provide a filename. When you click the Save button, Publisher then saves your website in Publisher format (.pub).

In the Save As dialog box, next to the Save button, you can click the down-arrow and choose the Save with Backup command to create a backup copy of your file.

To convert a web publication to a print publication, open the File menu, click Convert to Print Publication and follow the instructions given in the wizard.

Getting from Publisher format to web-ready format

At this stage, your website is not in web-ready format. When you publish your website to the web or network, Publisher creates a copy of your website and converts the copy to web-ready format (filtered HTML).

When you have published your website to the web, consider whether to submit it to the main search engines. However, be careful how you perform website submissions. Make sure you do not break any search engine rules. More information about this important topic is available in Web Page Design in easy steps, also from this series.

However, when working on updates to your website, always keep a master .pub copy and work in Publisher format first. Then, when ready, republish your web page(s) and upload to your web space. If you make changes to your website in Publisher but can't see those changes on your live website, remember, you'll need to republish your updated website – then you'll see the latest web pages.

Creating web page forms

Web page forms are often considered as challenging to set up. However, Publisher has made creating and manipulating web page forms easy. In this chapter, we cover the essentials and suggest some actions to take if your web form doesn't appear to give the results you expect.

Covers

Chapter Thirteen

Introduction to web page forms

A web page form is the electronic equivalent of a paper-based form. But a web form can be much more valuable. Web forms are an ideal addition to a website if you want to gain important information and make the job of submitting information easy for your visitors.

When using text labels for the components of your form, keep to simple, easy-to-understand words to make the job of filling in a form online quick and easy for your customers and visitors.

Creating a form: your two choices

You can use one of the predesigned forms in the Design Gallery. Publisher provides three basic designs: an Order form, a Response form and a Sign-up form. You might need to modify the chosen form to meet with your precise requirements and in Publisher, this is easy to do. Alternatively, you can design and create a form entirely from scratch.

What makes up a web form

Publisher provides the following seven types of components that can be used to make up a form:

Every web form must contain a Submit button – or equivalent. Although the name may be different, the commands associated with this type of button establish where to send the data gathered by the form.

Check box

List box (one choice from the list)

Single-line text box

Multiple-line text box

A Reset button allows a visitor to clear a form, if they change their mind or make a mistake, and want to start entering data again.

Option button (one option)

Submit command button (essential)

Reset command button (optional)

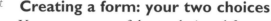

Using a predesigned web page form

Here's one way to add one of Publisher's predesigned forms to a web page. On the Objects toolbar (shown below), click the Design Gallery Object button: Then, continue with the steps below:

A key point about designing a web form, is that it should be quick and easy for your visitors to complete. If not, many may not bother, unless you offer some compelling reason for them to submit the form.

1 In the Design Gallery dialog box, click the Objects by Category tab.

2 Under Categories, click Reply Forms.

3 Under Reply Forms, double-click the form you want, or select the form you want and click the Insert Object button.

You can create a form from scratch using the Form Control button on the Objects toolbar:

Click this button to display a floating menu containing access to the main types of component that you can use. Click your desired component, then click on the page where you want to place the component. Finally, edit to fine-tune the placement and labelling of each component used.

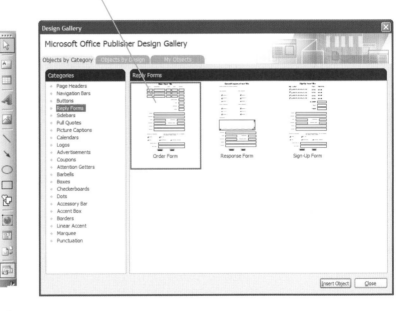

When you position a form object on the page, make sure the form doesn't touch other adjacent objects on the page. If another object overlaps onto the form, the form controls may not function properly. Ideally, allow a clear area of free space around a web form.

4 Carefully drag the form object onto the page and into position.

5 Now double-click and set up each form control component as required. Read the rest of this chapter to understand more about working with form components.

6 (Optional) Add, edit or reformat any other parts of the form, like titles, section names, and so on, as you want.

Web page form controls explained

Web form controls are the various boxes and buttons via which a visitor may enter some information and then send it somewhere else. The seven web form controls are:

- TextBox: allows for up to one line of typed information

- Text Area: allows for several lines of typed information

- List Box: presents several options in a list. A visitor can scroll down the list to highlight or select one or more options

- Check box: provides several independent choices that are part of a related group. If multiple check boxes are provided, a visitor can select several

- Option buttons: indicates a Yes or No choice. If several option buttons are used together in a related group, only one can be selected at a time

- Submit button: determines what happens to the information in the form, and where it is sent. Every web page form must have a Submit button. May be called by other names like "Send" or "Order Now", and so on

- Reset button: provides a one-click way to erase all previously entered information in a web page form, and allow a visitor to re-enter their data. A Reset button is optional

Adding labels and values to your form controls

Every form control needs a label (name) and a value (what is returned when a visitor sends the form). For example, an online credit card payment form might have five option buttons to represent the method of payment with labels such as: Check, Bill me, Visa, MasterCard, and American Express.

Imagine the Visa option button is selected. When the visitor clicks the Submit button, the information returned under a label called MethodOfPayment could be: Check = No, Bill me = No, Visa = Yes, MasterCard = No, American Express = No.

So in this example, the web page form recipient would immediately know that the method of payment for this communication is Visa.

Establishing your web form properties

Although the example procedure below refers to a check box, similar procedures also apply to adding option buttons, TextBox, list box, and so on.

To add a web form control to a check box (example)

On the Objects toolbar, click Form Control, followed by Checkbox. Publisher places the check box form control onto the page. Drag the form control where you want. Double-click the checkbox form control. In the Checkbox Properties dialog box, under Data processing, in Return data with this label box, type the label you want to use. Under Data processing, in the Checkbox value box, type the value you want to use. Click OK to finish.

Typically, if you are using your Internet Service Provider (ISP) or web host to process or store the information received from your web form, you may also need to use hidden fields. Your ISP or web host can advise what names to use and value to apply. To learn more about using hidden fields, type "hidden fields" into Publisher Help Search box and press Enter.

Processing the form data

You can see the options available by double-clicking the Submit button, followed by Form Properties. Publisher then displays the Form Properties dialog box. You have three options:

- save the form data in a file stored on the web server. Note: the web server must support Microsoft FrontPage server extensions

- have the form data sent to you by e-mail. Note: your Internet service provider must support Microsoft FrontPage 98 version 3.0, or later server extensions

- collect the form data using a program from your Internet Service Provider (ISP). Discuss this option with your ISP or website host to determine what values you need

Laying out your form controls inline

Sometimes, web page forms can be particularly difficult to use for physically challenged users. Also, in many countries, website accessibility is at last gaining the recognition it deserves, so a variety of guidelines, suggestions, directives and disability standards are emerging.

One way to help physically challenged users navigate your web page forms more easily, is to create and place form controls inline. Then, your visitor can use the Tab key to step through and select each form control as required. Perform the steps below:

When you insert your form controls, you can place them on the same line horizontally, leave a space, then insert the next form control. Or, to place vertically, press Enter after inserting each form control.

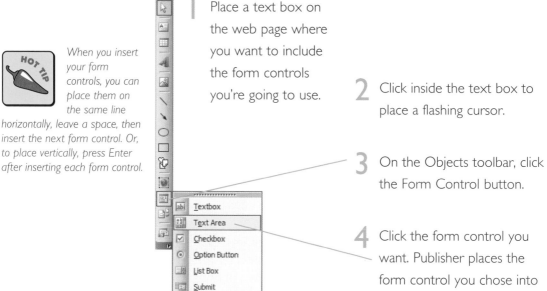

1 Place a text box on the web page where you want to include the form controls you're going to use.

2 Click inside the text box to place a flashing cursor.

3 On the Objects toolbar, click the Form Control button.

4 Click the form control you want. Publisher places the form control you chose into the text box.

5 Repeat Steps 2 – 4 to insert all the form controls you want. See margin tip for layout.

6 When finished, open the File menu and click Web Page Preview, to view your web page form in your default web browser. Press Tab to step through the form controls. You can press the Arrow keys to move through groups of option buttons.

Testing your web page form

Once your web page form has been created and is live, before promoting and advertising, perform a few basic checks to ensure that your form performs as you expect.

First, connect to the Internet. In your web browser, enter the web address of your web page form. Save this as a Favorite, for easy access later. When you see your web page form, make a visual check to ensure the form reads correctly and that form controls are where you expect them to be. Ideally, use several different web browsers to check your form.

Next, perform a test booking or registration. Type in your information into every field. Also, write what you enter so that you can compare notes later when you receive the electronic copy. Double-check that each page control performs properly. Test the Reset button if one is included in your web page form. Then, re-enter the information you have written down. When ready, click the Submit button.

Go to where your form data is being received and verify that you have received it. Compare the information received with your written notes. Correct any errors, then perform the above steps again. When satisfied, publish your web page form.

Repairing a broken web page form

Consider the following guidelines if you experience problems with your web page form.

Problem: my web form doesn't appear to send back any information. Remedy suggestions:

- check that you are using the latest web page form. If you performed some updates to your Publisher form, ensure that you have generated an updated form and uploaded or published the new web form to your web space

- press the Refresh button in your web browser

- make sure that your destination settings are configured correctly

- if you are using an option that requires Microsoft FrontPage Extensions, make sure that your web host or ISP has the correct versions installed and set up

- check e-mail addresses and web addresses carefully

- if you used any hidden fields specified by your web host or ISP, make sure that these names and values are correct

Problem: the information I receive from my form isn't clear. Remedy suggestions:

- consider renaming some of the labels used

- re-check the values you set originally

Problem: some information that I receive is missing. Remedy suggestions:

- perhaps your visitor simply forgot to fill in all the required fields

- or, check that any grouped form controls like check boxes and option buttons have been set up properly, and that they use separate, unique identifiers

Previewing and publishing your website

This chapter outlines how to check for errors, view your website in web browser, then bring it to life by publishing to the web or your organization's network – whether it's for the first time, or a regular update.

Covers

Chapter Fourteen

Creating accessible websites

An accessible website helps able-bodied and physically challenged users to use it more easily. Consider these guidelines:

To create good color contrast, consider using dark-colored text on a light-colored background. However, for some disabilities, yellow text on a black background has been shown to be especially useful. Therefore: take some time to learn about your key visitors.

Physically challenged visitors may use a range of accessibility aids when using the Internet or working with a computer. Examples could include: screen-driven keyboards, screen readers and speech recognition software. By following the design guidelines on this page, you can help improve the accessibility of your website.

For more information, visit the following websites:

1. Section 508 Requirements: www.section508.gov/final_text.html
2. World Wide Web Consortium Web Accessibility Initiative: www.w3c.org/WAI/
3. http://colorfilter.wickline.org
4. www.rnib.org.uk/
5. http://bobby.watchfire.com/bobby/

- arguably, the most important rule: ensure that all text and graphics can be understood easily. Make sure there is good color contrast between text and the web page background. Essential: see margin tips. Observe any legal requirements

- avoid using a complex patterned web page background

- make your default body text size at least 10 points in size. Ensure that text size can be changed if necessary by a visitor using the commands in their web browser

- use only fonts that are designed for a website and which have been chosen especially for screen use. For example: Arial, Verdana and Georgia

- whenever you include a picture or graphic component in your website, make sure you also include alternative (ALT) text that briefly describes the picture or graphic. Alternative text can help visitors who use screen readers to better understand a website. See page 156 for more information

- make sure that the text you choose for each hyperlink makes sense and gives a clue as to where the hyperlink is pointing and what the topic is about. If possible, also include a descriptive title for a hyperlink

- include a website navigation bar or set of buttons that help a visitor to easily move around your website. For maximum compatibility, use a text-only navigation bar, rather than buttons alone – or include both

- Ensure that your website can be navigated using a keyboard, using the Tab, Arrows and Enter keys

- if you include web forms, lay out your form controls inline as outlined on page 168. Also, give a meaningful label to each form control you use

Using Design Checker in web mode

Design Checker can help you identify any web layout or design problems. Always run Design Checker at least once, before you publish a website. With your web publication open, first, open the Tools menu and click Design Checker. Publisher displays the Design Checker task pane, checks your web publication, and lists any errors found. Under Select an item to fix, click the down-arrow next to the first error you want to fix. You then have four options:

- to move to the page on which this current problem is situated, click Go to this Item

- to have Publisher automatically fix the current problem, click Fix:automatic. The name Publisher may give to an automatic fix depends on the nature of the problem. Often, an automatic fix is not available

- to have Publisher not check for this type of problem again, click Never Run this Check Again

- to have Publisher display an appropriate Help topic that contains further guidelines and help, click Explain

Repeat, the above steps to fix every error found.

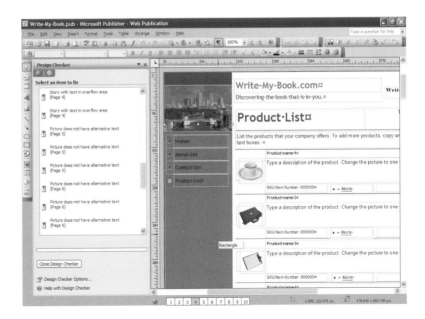

Previewing your website

Once you have created your masterpiece, run the Design Checker and carried out spell-checking and proofreading tasks, you can preview your website using a web browser installed on your PC. This will show how your website will appear when you publish to the web, and will also allow you to test the hyperlinks and to check that each hyperlink points to the address you want.

Use the spell checker and other proofreading tools and tips outlined in this book, to help check your website for these types of errors before publishing.

To preview your website, first, open the File menu, and click Web Page Preview, or click the Web Page Preview button on the Standard toolbar: 🔍 Then, make sure that the general look and feel is as you expect. Check that your text size is not too small (or too large). Make sure all the hyperlinks work correctly; also check that any e-mail links work as expected. If you have included any sound components, you'll need to ensure that these too work as you expect.

Before publishing your website to the WWW, confirm your designs and highlight any problem areas using the Design Checker, as described earlier in this chapter.

If you find any errors, make a note of each error and continue your checks. Then go back to your Publisher file and correct the mistakes. Repeat these preview steps again. When you're satisfied that everything is working correctly on your local web browser, you're ready to publish your website or web pages to the web as outlined in the following pages. Later, you can also check your web pages live after publishing on the web.

If, when you preview your web pages, the layout seems incorrect, make sure you are using the latest version of the Microsoft Internet Explorer web browser. Some older versions may not be able to interpret today's web pages correctly. Remedy: upgrade your web browser.

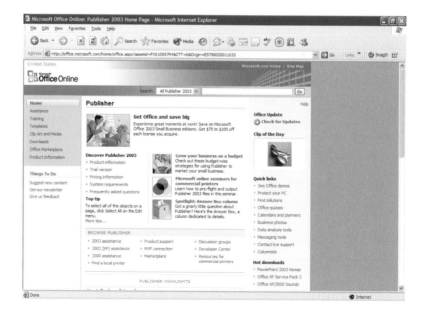

Three ways to publish your website

Publisher provides three options to publish a website:

- publish directly to the web, or to an organization's network Intranet. For web publishing, you must already have Internet access and web hosting space ready to use – see page 176

- upload your website using File Transfer Protocol (FTP) – see page 177

- publish your website to a folder on your PC, and transfer it to the web or Intranet later – see page 178

Before performing the steps outlined in this chapter, always ask your ISP about what you need to do to publish your website. Why? Some ISPs may have their own software and web publishing procedures that you must follow instead.

What is filtered HTML?

When you save a website file, Publisher saves your website in its native .pub format. For example, you may call your first website company-name-v1.pub.

However, when you choose to publish your website, using the Publish to the Web command in the File menu, Publisher creates a new copy of each page and saves it in a special filtered HTML format, to help speed up actual web publishing later. Publisher refers to the copied format as filtered HTML.

If you can't upload your web page files to a website now, you can publish your website to a folder on your computer instead, then manually upload the files later, as outlined starting on page 178.

In Publisher, you can't edit a web page that has been saved in filtered HTML format.

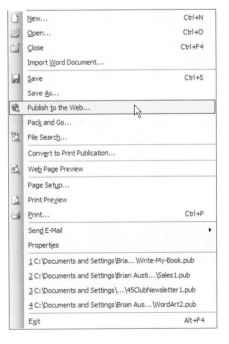

Therefore, to make updates to a website, you must work on the original website in its native .pub format. Then republish your updated website again, creating updated pages in filtered HTML format, ready for the web.

Updating your website is covered in more detail on page 179.

Publishing to the web or a network

Before attempting to publish a website to a corporate Intranet, ask your system administrator what steps you need to take to publish your web pages. Why? You may have to save your web pages in a specific format and use a different procedure to that outlined on this page, before you can successfully publish it.

Before you publish to the web, make sure that you have obtained suitable web hosting space. Most Internet Service Providers (ISPs) now make available a certain amount of free web space with your account. When you rent web space from a web hosting company, an ISP, or are publishing to an organization's Intranet, you need several information snippets before you start, including:

- the web address or URL (see second margin tip) to which you must publish your web pages or website

- optionally the user name and password of the location above

With the web address you need to hand, to publish a website to the web or to an organization's network, first open the File menu and click Publish to the Web.

Next, in the Publish to the Web dialog box, type the URL into the File name box, then click Save.

Another name for a web address is a Uniform Resource Locator (URL). A URL states a protocol (examples include: HTTP or FTP), plus where an item or publications is located. An example URL is: http://www.ineasysteps.com/

If Publisher prompts you to enter the user name and password, do so, then click OK. When you see the destination directory in the Publish to the Web dialog box, double-click the folder you want. In the File name box, choose index as the name of your Home page. Click Save. Click OK to finish.

A more formal name for the web is World Wide Web (WWW). The web is the most popular branch of the Internet. The Internet is the name given to millions of computers and computer groups around the world, that connect and share information.

![Publish to the Web dialog box showing the Websites folder with files 45ClubNewsletter 1PNG, index_files, and index.htm. The File name field contains http://www.internettips.com/public_html and Save as type is set to Web Page, Filtered (*.htm;*.html).]

Publishing to the web using FTP

Before starting the steps below, contact you ISP, web hosting company or system administrator, and note down the settings you'll need. For example, if publishing to the web host, you would be given a FTP website name, a user name and a password. Open the File menu and click Publish to the Web. Now perform the steps below:

1 In the Publish to the Web dialog box, in the Save in box, click FTP Locations.

2 Double-click Add/Modify FTP Locations.

3 Type in the information your ISP made available, then click OK, followed by Cancel.

If you originally used FTP to upload your website, you can simply use the same method for updating it. For more advice and information, contact your ISP.

4 Open the File menu again and click Publish to the Web again.

5 Next, in the Save in box, click FTP Locations.

6 Look at the list of FTP websites shown in the dialog box. Double-click the FTP location you want.

7 Double-click the destination folder you want

8 Click Save.

Publishing a local copy website

If you're not ready yet to publish your website to the web, or to a company Intranet, you can instead publish all of your website files to a single convenient folder on your computer. Then later, you can upload your website pages to their final location. To publish your website to a folder, after saving your website file, first open the File menu and click Publish to the Web. Then follow the steps below.

1 In the Publish to the Web dialog box, in the Save in box, move to the drive or folder where you want to publish your website files.

2 Then perform Step 3 or Step 4 before going on to Step 5.

3 Double-click the folder you want.

4 Click Create New folder, and type a name for your new folder in the Name box.

5 Type a file name for the home page of your website.

6 Click Save to finish.

Checking and updating your website

To check your live website

After you have published your website on the web, consider the following guidelines:

- immediately check your website using at least one web browser (preferably two different browsers)

- have note paper and pencil handy, then check each page. Make a note of any errors to be fixed

- look at layout, read all the text and make sure all the images appear correct

- double-check that all the hyperlinks go to where they should and test any e-mail hyperlinks

- if you have included any sound components, make sure they run correctly

- try out any web forms you created, and make sure you can correctly access or receive the web page form data that you enter in your test

To update your website

Updating your website is easy in Publisher. Simply open your original Publisher file (.pub), make your latest changes and re-save. Then, publish your updated website again as outlined on the previous pages, with just a few minor differences.

Once you publish your website to the web or to an organization's network, In My Network Places, Publisher places a Windows short-cut either to the web server or the network server to which you publish.

Therefore, to update, first open the File menu, and click the Publish to the Web command. In the Publish to the Web dialog box, this time click My Network Places.

Next, look for the short-cut to the web server folder or network server folder, where you previously published your website; double-click the short-cut. In the File name box, type the filename of the file you want to update. Then, double-click the folder in which you want to save your file. Click Save to finish updating.

To change your incremental website publishing settings

Incremental website publishing can ensure that when you publish updates to a website, only the changed files get updated, not the entire website. The key benefit of incremental web publishing is that this feature can save you time. By default, incremental publishing is turned on in Publisher.

Here's how incremental web publishing works. Imagine you created a website in Publisher and published to the website space using the Publish to the Web command in the File menu.

When you next come to update the Publisher source file, then republish to the web with incremental publishing turned on, Publisher will only publish the updated web pages, saving considerable time.

However, if you want to work on your website directly on the web server, this is one instance in which you may want to turn off incremental publishing. Open the Tools menu, and click Options followed by the Web tab. Under the Saving section, to turn incremental publishing off, deselect the Enable incremental publish to the Web check box. Click OK.

If you want to enable incremental publishing, perform the same steps as outlined in the previous paragraph, except this time, click the check box: Enable incremental publish to the Web, to place a tick mark in the box. Then click OK to finish.

Research and translation services

If you've read this book from the start, you've come a long way: congratulations!
In this chapter, we finish by exploring the amazingly versatile research and
translation tools in Microsoft Office. Now you can use these expert tools to
help deliver a polished finish to any desktop published document or website you
may create in Publisher.

Covers

Chapter Fifteen

Introducing research services

Now, without leaving Office Publisher, you can research or find information from a range of sources on the Internet, and better locate the information you want stored on your own computer. Research services available from the Research task pane include:

Research services are also available in a range of other Microsoft Office 2003 (and related) programs.

- Dictionary: from Microsoft Encarta containing around 400,000 entries – plus world history notes, and pronunciation aids. Additional, compatible dictionaries may also be added and used

- Thesaurus: find words that have a similar meaning

- Encyclopedia: get answers to questions that you ask in Microsoft Encarta online, and gain access to over 42,000 articles. See additional links to related sources

After you have started Research, and performed several tasks, to quickly go back to results or information accessed in the current research session, you can click the Back and Forward buttons in the Research task pane to find the result or query you want.

- Translation: gain access to bilingual dictionaries to help makes sense of words and phrases. Or use direct web machine translation to translate a phrase, paragraph or an entire document (see margin)

- MSN Web search: for easy access to one of the web's most popular search engines

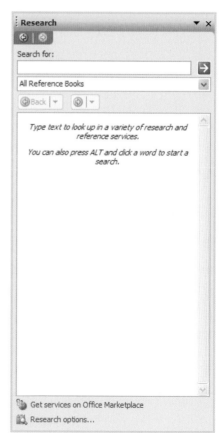

Machine translation may not produce perfect results. For important projects, consider discussing the results with a qualified translator.

- Stock quotes and company information: enter a stock symbol, company name or a few relevant search words, and check out a company as you work in Publisher

- Additional third-party services: such as additional translation options from WorldLingo, eLibrary (news and periodical features), news from Factiva, and company information from Gale

- Services from Intranet websites to which you have authorized access: simply add your Intranet to the Research task pane here (see first margin tip)

To access research services

Open the Tools menu and click Research, to have display the Research task pane.

If you're not sure how to spell a word, simply type the first few characters of the word you want in the Search for box, and press Enter.

To turn on password-protected parental control

Open the Tools menu, click Research. Then, click Research options. In the Research Options dialog box, choose the options you want. Click the Parental Control button, then in the Parental Control dialog box, click the check box, plus choose any other options you want, including entering a password if desired. Click OK twice.

To add research services

Display the Research Options dialog box as outlined in the previous section. Connect to the

Research options you choose are not fixed: you can add or change research services at any time. Plus, you can also set up password-controlled parental access, to help filter out unsuitable information on the Internet or on web pages that you do not want to be seen.

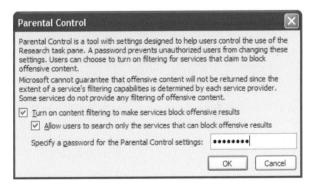

Internet, then click the Add Services button. Select the options you want and click Add.

To update or remove research services

Display the Research Options dialog box as outlined in "To turn on password-protected parental control". To update some research services, you'll need to be connected to the Internet. Click the Update/Remove button and select the service you want to update or remove. Click either Update or Remove, depending on which you want. Click Close to finish.

Using Microsoft Encarta encyclopedia

If you want to use Microsoft Encarta encyclopedia, remember, first connect to the Internet before performing the steps below.

1 Open the Tools menu and click Research.

2 In the Search for list, choose Encarta Encyclopedia: English (North America).

3 Now perform Step 4, Step 5, or Step 6, before going to Step 7.

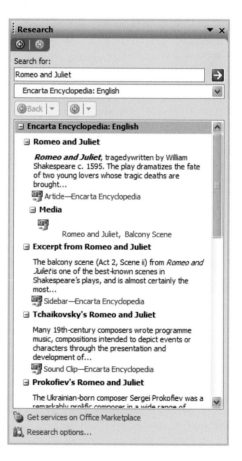

4 To search using a single word, press and hold down Alt, then click the word you want.

5 To search using a phrase, first select the words you want, press and hold down Alt, then click the phrase you selected.

6 Or, type the word or phrase you want in the Search for box.

7 Click the Start Searching button to see your results in the lower part of the Research task pane.

Using Office translation services

Microsoft Office 2003 includes powerful translation services that can use bilingual dictionaries stored on your computer and on the web. For more in-depth translation projects, you can also consider using Publisher's web-based machine translation tools.

To use translation services

First, make sure you're connected to the Internet, or you may be prompted to connect later. Internet-based research services extend the power of Publisher, when it cannot find the results you want from the records or tools installed on your own computer.

If you are online, but Publisher prompts you to connect to the Internet, check the status of your Work Offline command in the File menu of your Microsoft Internet Explorer web browser. If "Work Offline" has a tick mark next to the command, Publisher may consider this to mean "not connected to the Internet". In that event, click Work Offline to turn on your web browser.

For simple translation, press and hold down the Alt key, then click a word in your publication to have Publisher provide a translation in the Research task pane.

If you access more complex machine translation on the web, you can have paragraphs, sections or an entire publication translated – possibly an ideal option if the content of your publication is simple in nature, and does not contain any ambiguous words or phrases.

Language is complex, which can lead to imprecise translations, if we rely on machine translation alone. Therefore, when working with important documents, certainly ask a competent language translator to examine your translated document and make any changes necessary.

How to translate text

Step-by-step Microsoft Office text translation
Perform the steps below:

The bilingual dictionaries that come with, or which can be accessed through Publisher, can be useful for the translation of basic words and brief phrases. Consider using online machine translation services for longer sections or when seeking translation of more complex material (see margin tips below).

1 Open the Tools menu and click Research. Publisher displays the Research task pane.

2 In the Search for list, click Translation. If you have not used translation services before, Publisher may ask to install bilingual dictionaries and activate translation services, so click OK if necessary.

3 Choose the language you want to translate from and the language you want to translate to, in the From and To boxes, respectively. Then, select the options you want.

4 (Optional) To see more options, click Translation options, choose the additional options you want and then click OK.

Depending on which languages you are working with, Publisher or Windows may prompt you to install additional modules relating to the languages you want to work with.

5 Now, perform Step 6, Step 7, Step 8, or Step 9, depending on what you want, to have Publisher display the results in the task pane.

6 To translate a single word, press and hold down Alt and click the word you want.

The range and the scope of languages spoken is mind-boggling. Microsoft Office translation services may perform adequately when working on some publications for some languages. Discuss your important projects with a language translator who is a specialist in the target language.

7 To translate a phrase or sentence, highlight the words or sentence you want, then press and hold down Alt and click the words you highlighted.

8 To translate an entire publication, if available, click Translate whole document.

9 If you want to translate a single word or phrase, you can also type the word or phrase in the Search for box and click Start Searching.

Index

L

M

N

O

T

U

W

Z